THE ART OF REVOLT

THE ART OF REVOLT

SNOWDEN, ASSANGE, MANNING

GEOFFROY DE LAGASNERIE

STANFORD UNIVERSITY PRESS • STANFORD, CALIFORNIA

**303.
61
LAG**

Stanford University Press
Stanford, California

The Art of Revolt: Snowden, Assange, Manning was originally published in French in 2015 under the title *L'art de la révolte: Snowden, Assange, Manning* © Librairie Arthème Fayard 2015.

Printed in the United States of America on acid-free, archival-quality paper

Library of Congress Cataloging-in-Publication Data

Names: Lagasnerie, Geoffroy de, author.
Title: The art of revolt : Snowden, Assange, Manning / Geoffroy de Lagasnerie.
Other titles: Art de la révolte. English
Description: Stanford, California : Stanford University Press, 2017. |
    Translation of: L'art de la révolte. | Includes bibliographical references.
Identifiers: LCCN 2016059143 (print) | LCCN 2017006514 (ebook) |
    ISBN 9781503600010 (cloth : alk. paper) | ISBN 9781503603325 (pbk. : alk.
    paper) | ISBN 9781503603240 (e-book)
Subjects: LCSH: Government, Resistance to. | Snowden, Edward J., 1983– |
    Assange, Julian. | Manning, Chelsea, 1987– | WikiLeaks (Organization)
Classification: LCC JC328.3 .L3313 2017 (print) | LCC JC328.3 (ebook) |
    DDC 303.6/10922—dc23
LC record available at https://lccn.loc.gov/2016059143

Typeset by Bruce Lundquist in 10/15 Adobe Garamond Pro

CONTENTS

THE ART OF REVOLT

SOMETHING IS HAPPENING

ONLY RARELY does something *new* emerge in the political sphere. Of course, this is not to say that radical questions or movements arise infrequently. By good fortune, new matters of contestation, new sources of outrage, and therefore new battles unfold without end in the social world. As they do, they enlarge the sphere of liberty, equality, and social justice for each one of us.

All the same, the proliferation—the sheer number—of fields of engagement cannot hide the fact that most of the time such mobilization takes place within standing traditions. Battles proceed according to established forms. In the main, the vocabularies, values, and objectives at stake are predetermined; they are not a matter of choice even for the actors themselves. Institutions structure the time and space of protest.

Paradoxically, perhaps, politics represents one of the most codified domains of social life. We live and come into our subjective own in a given environment. Political activity entails taking up preexisting forms, situating ourselves in an inherited framework, and negotiating with and within these structures in order to achieve a specific objective at a given moment. Strikes, demonstrations, petitions, lobbying, riots, and so on represent institutionalized modes of protest (what the social sciences, following Charles Tilly, now call "repertoires of collective action"[1]). Even the most radical claims cannot escape these conditions, which mark out and define the terrain of democracy. It is by virtue of being inscribed in preexisting frames of contention that political action is evident as such; in accepting these frames, the subject stands as a citizen taking part in communal deliberation. Conversely, as soon as a struggle fails to bow to prescribed forms of expression, it proves controversial: debate arises about whether a given movement is "criminal," "terrorist," or "political" in nature.

By the same token, the framework that prevails in the political sphere permeates our minds and determines our ways of seeing. The difficulty of assigning a place to something new in the political realm may also be explained by the fact that, when a singular movement emerges, the odds are that it will not be recognized for what it is. Its specificity and unprecedented character derail categories of perception and therefore escape notice. Movements of this kind often wind up being explained, even by those actively pursuing them, by way of preexisting terminologies rather than being grasped as original.

Theoretical interpretations of political movements tend to take up a fixed vocabulary. Struggles are reinscribed in a history, a tradition; in consequence, the stakes are recoded to correspond to an existing paradigm. The stance adopted by intellectuals, philosophers, and even historians frequently leads to the colonization of struggles, in which an outdated structure is imposed on them. Against this propensity toward totalization, generalization, and universalization, critical analysis needs to operate in terms of singularity, specificity, and therefore rupture.

Novelty

The thesis I would like to advance is that *we are now witnessing something emerging* around the figures of Edward Snowden, Julian Assange, and Chelsea Manning. A new way of thinking and conducting politics—of conceiving forms and practices of resistance—is in the process of crystallizing. The battles currently taking shape around state secrets, mass surveillance, the protection of privacy, and civil liberties in the Internet age pose new problems. In the book at hand, they serve as the point of departure for critical reflection on the possibility of thinking and acting otherwise.

Snowden, Assange, and Manning should not be seen simply as whistle-blowers, whose activities involved the diffusion of information. They are much more than that. Here, they will be treated as activists, exemplary figures bringing a new political art into existence: a different way of understanding what it means to resist. Their actions, their very lives, express something that must be heard and heeded: the advent of a new political subject.

In other words, the cases of Snowden, Assange, and Manning do not just bring new political objectives to light. It is not simply a matter of new points of dissent arising and coming to occupy the public spotlight. Rather, what we are seeing are new modes of subjectification. These three figures are not just interrogating events within the political landscape and how those events unfold: they are throwing the political landscape itself into crisis.

Reaction

Indeed, how else can one even explain the violence of governmental responses to their actions other than in terms of the radical destabilization they have effected? Their activities (but also, it is important to note, the activities of other whistle-blowers and hackers who remain less well-known) have unleashed repressive measures of a rare intensity. Especially in the United States, the call for punishment has assumed unprecedented, extraordinary, and, all in all, fundamentally incomprehensible dimensions. The American justice system went after Manning simply for having published confidential documents, some of which revealed illegal government and military activities. The prosecutor sought a sentence of sixty years, for treason;[2] ultimately, Manning was sentenced to thirty-five. In pre-trial custody, she was locked in a cell for twenty-three hours a day, without a pillow or sheets, and forbidden any exercise (a guard stood watch the whole time[3]). In the United States, WikiLeaks—which merely hosts a space for publishing reports—has been put into the legal category of "enemies of the state" (like al-Qaeda or the Taliban, according to *The Sydney Morning Herald*). Julian Assange, and anyone else who contributes to the organization, potentially faces the charge of "collaboration with the enemy"—in other words, the prospect of being brought before a military tribunal and sentenced to death.[4] For having alerted the public to the National Security Agency (NSA)'s (often illegal) surveillance programs involving mass monitoring of citizens the world over and of certain heads of state and diplomats, Edward Snowden was charged with espionage; he still faces the risk of a military trial and a lifelong prison sentence. The United States government has made every diplomatic effort to ensuring that he will not escape its justice by obtaining asylum in another country.

Whether in terms of rhetoric ("cowards," "enemies," "spies," "traitors," etc.), charges brought ("treason," "aiding and abetting the enemy"), sentences sought and/or imposed, or conditions of detention, we are witnessing a veritable spectacle of the state's repressive apparatus in all its uncompromising brutality. This penal violence and this disproportionate reaction are significant in their own right and should prompt us to ask about how the contemporary political and legal order operates. These repressive measures are not severe because the "crimes" are serious: they are severe because so-called whistle-blowers profoundly unsettle the legal and political regime, the framework of the state. (The situation may be understood in terms of how states are now reacting to the progressive erosion of national order and territorial sovereignty by ostentatiously building impressive walls at their borders.[5]) The task, then, is to study this destabilization, its reasons and form, in order to grasp its true significance and dimensions.

Homage

This book is meant to pay homage to the gestures and lives of Edward Snowden, Julian Assange, and Chelsea Manning. Its point of departure does not lie on any theoretical or political plane but stems instead from a kind of admiration for the course they have steered—as well as a feeling of indignation, and even anger, at the measures taken (and still being taken) against them.

When one starts writing for such reasons, it is important to know what role to give to one's anger and admiration—that is, how to use them. What does it mean to write a book fueled by indignation? Above all, how can one avoid remaining stuck in an emotional register? How is it possible to ensure that the text does not merely express spontaneous emotions to buttress existing perceptions?

For me, paying homage to the actions of Snowden, Assange, and Manning means not attempting to be an advocate for their ideas. Reformulating how they have accounted for themselves, their motivations, would mean assuming a subordinate role; it would entail giving up on what gives theoretical reflection its significance: the capacity to transform set ways of seeing and thinking. Instead, I have sought to draw inspiration from their energy, their resolve. In a sense, they have served as models; the task is to prove as radical, in terms of theory, as they have been in terms of politics. To display intellectual loyalty to Snowden, Assange, and Manning, one must offer a theory commensurate with the heights their concrete engagements have attained.

For the same reason, what follows will not necessarily agree with what they themselves say, or have said. My project may be considered structural or objectivist in inspiration. The aim is to start with

Snowden, Assange, and Manning and the struggles taking shape around their persons and activities in order to extract from these spheres of action an internal and immanent realm of positivity: a realm that exists unbeknownst even to those implicated in it. To be sure, Snowden, Assange, and Manning are different people who understand the significance of their activities in divergent terms (and needless to say, the same holds for hackers, the Anonymous collective, and so on). But notwithstanding the readily apparent differences between these individuals and their motivations, there is an overall coherence that can be discerned in the actions they have performed. I hope to reconstitute this coherence in a way that is similar to the method used by Michel Foucault in *The Order of Things*. Foucault demonstrates how a single, objective movement, namely dissolving the category of "man," is at work in three separate realms within the regime of knowledge—the three counter-sciences of ethnology, linguistics, and psychoanalysis—and that this movement signals the advent of a new episteme, whose nature eludes each of these sciences (and their practitioners) in isolation.[6]

Snowden, Assange, and Manning are the protagonists of a movement that is questioning the very ground we stand on, the mechanisms that define our present. As such, they enable us both to think in a new way and to interrogate received ways of thinking. Their very lives invite us to imagine other modes of relation to the law, the nation, citizenship, and so forth.

Along those lines, this book proposes a critical exchange with the most important analyses of power and sovereignty in contemporary discourse—to formulate a set of questions about obedience and citizenship in relation to the state, the nation, the law, democracy, and so on. My aim is to investigate our political unconscious, to examine existing modes of political subjectification and their limits, in order to envision practical action—modes and forms of engagement, resistance, and sedition—in a new and different way.

Sites

Needless to say, I am well aware that other theorists have identified other movements and mobilizations as the sites of political renewal. Authors such as Judith Butler, Noam Chomsky, Angela Davis, Wendy Brown, Gayatri Spivak, and David Graeber privilege large-scale protests and popular assemblies: Occupy Wall Street; *Los indignados* in Spain; the Arab Spring, especially in Tunisia and Egypt; massive protests taking place in Turkey. . . .

Zuccotti Park in New York, Tahrir Square in Cairo, and Gezi Park in Istanbul have emerged as the symbolic spaces for mobilization that, it seems, should command our attention when trying to reconstitute an analysis of questions of democracy, capitalism, inequality, globalization, social justice, and so on.

I do not of course deny the importance of these movements and gatherings. That would prove pointless as it is uninteresting. To be sure, all serious intellectual efforts should take into account what these events have embodied. All the same, I submit that the scattered and solitary actions of Snowden, Assange, and Manning—to say nothing of those of certain hackers and whistle-blowers—have proven just as reinvigorating, innovative, and political. (What is more, we should ask what implicit conception of politics and resistance is being enlisted when we spontaneously accord greater "value" to large mobilizations on a public square than to the lone efforts of a hacker.) These individuals were and are scattered. They act not in concert, but rather in isolation. Still, the virtual collective they incarnate represents one of the essential sites for reformulating contemporary politics and renewing the demand for democracy.

This book might stand as the square where these actors are welcomed, that gathers them together. In assembling them in this way, it hopes to contribute to the questioning of our theoretical language, in order to arrive at a greater understanding of what democratic politics can mean.

PART I

CONDITIONS AND CIRCUMSTANCES

CHAPTER 1

DEMOCRACY, PRIVACY, AND CIVIL LIBERTIES

IN MAKING THE ACTIONS of Snowden, Assange, and Manning (and the mobilizations to which they give rise) the object of theoretical reflection, one faces a theoretical and political scene that is already well defined. The names of these figures are shorthand for a struggle that has been unfolding on an international scale for years: the defense of civil liberties and the rule of law against the tendency, on the part of governments, to dismantle these same structures in this "War on Terror" era. Understanding what is happening today—and grasping the interpretations that have already been offered—requires, above all else, that we take stock of the scope and stakes of what Snowden, Assange, and Manning have brought to light. It seems to me that the dimensions and radical nature of the field they have disclosed are seldom fully appreciated: on the one hand there is the problem of surveillance, of privacy and its protection; on the other, there is the problem of state secrets and how the logic of the state bears on the demands of democracy. My aim in the following is to shift our perspective in order to obtain a different view of what is at stake on this battleground.

Freedoms, Private Life, and Surveillance

Edward Snowden's revelations thrust the matter of privacy—and, more broadly, the problematic nature of relations among the state, rights, and individual liberties—to center stage. From June 2013 on, Snowden effectively made the activities of the NSA and other intelligence services public. These documents show how the United States, in the name of combating terrorism and in violation of constitutional protections, set up a massive-scale data-gathering system that affects the American citizenry as a whole. And not only that, they reveal that the government intercepts communications from foreign diplomats and leaders—even when they serve ally states.

Snowden's leaks provoked profound disquiet inasmuch as they made plain the ongoing weakening—if not outright abolition—of the protections afforded to individual spaces in contemporary democracies. The state is increasingly installing systems of surveillance and data-gathering mechanisms that operate on an international level; this matter no longer concerns just individuals suspected of being involved in criminal or terrorist enterprises, but *everyone*. Anyone at all, the world over, is now exposed to the watchful eye of power: e-mails, telephone calls, and exchanges on social networks could be—or have long been—archived, collected, and examined by intelligence services, police agencies, and others.

The information available thanks to Snowden shows how, little by little, key achievements of nineteenth-century political liberalism are being undermined. In effect, one of the glories of liberalism is to have invented a state that places limits on itself and incorporates the capacity for self-contradiction by instituting a certain number of rights: the notions of "privacy," personal or otherwise, and "domicile" constitute legal and theoretical measures meant to ensure the integrity of social spheres from which the state excludes itself—or, more precisely, spheres that the state cannot enter except under limited conditions, strictly defined by law.

However, in our day and age, a new kind of political rationale is emerging, characterized by the fact that the state no longer accepts such restrictions. The state is expanding the field of intervention and dismantling the systems and guarantees that, until now, had impeded its intrusive logic. The threat of terrorism, hovering over the populace as a whole, is invoked to justify the unchecked authority to monitor, and intervene in, the lives of individuals. States—and especially the United States—consider everything as falling within their purview; nothing is allowed to remain foreign. This is the situation to which Glenn Greenwald, who used to work for the *Guardian* and who published Snowden's documents on NSA operations, was referring when he called his book *No Place to Hide*. The surveillance technologies being developed in the Internet age aim for conditions under which there would no longer be anything outside the state: the notion of "privacy" stands to become obsolete and fall apart.

Edward Snowden observed as much in a letter he addressed to journalists to explain his actions:

> My sole motive is to inform the public as to that which is done in their name and that which is done against them. The U.S. government, in conspiracy with client states, chiefest among them the Five Eyes—the United Kingdom, Canada, Australia, and New Zealand—have inflicted upon the world a system of secret, pervasive surveillance *from which there is no refuge*. They protect their domestic systems from the oversight of citizenry through classification and lies, and shield themselves from outrage in the event of leaks by overemphasizing limited protections they choose to grant the governed. . . .[1]

In seeking to alert the public to the fact that we inhabit a world increasingly commandeered by "omnipresent" and "omniscient"[2] mass surveillance, then, Snowden sought to revive a classic political question: the question of the ability of citizens to create spaces that escape state supervision and control. In other words, how is it possible to restore meaning to "privacy"? How, in the age of the Internet, can the power of the state be limited? How can we rethink arrangements for protecting individual liberties? How is it possible to resist the hegemonic tendencies of states—the right they arrogate to themselves to know everything about individuals, intruding into the most intimate spheres of life without legitimate cause?

One objective of the groups taking the field in this contested space—especially WikiLeaks, whose spokesman is Julian Assange, but also Anonymous—is to inform citizens about methods of encryption: everyone should be able to conceal private communications and hide his or her identity on the Internet, thereby escaping surveillance. The point is to democratize access to technology so that individuals can reconstitute, on their own, an autonomous sphere to which the state cannot gain entry: inasmuch as the law no longer blocks state intervention, it is incumbent on citizens to employ existing technological means to achieve this same end. The interesting thing here is that the critique of the technology used by states and intelligence services does not entail a critique of the Internet; on the contrary, it leads to enlisting the potential offered by digital communication in an even more radical manner. The will to reconstitute, against state intrusion, an "intimate" sphere—a sphere of "private life"—has not led to anti-technological discourse; it has not yielded to the reactionary temptation to go backwards, to withdraw from the technological world. Quite the contrary: it has given birth to a discourse and a praxis that call for still more technology, greater technical mastery. (In due course, I will show how such anonymity constitutes an extremely important locus of political invention.)

The Call for Democracy and State Logic

The defense of civil liberties is not limited to privacy issues or the creation of spheres exempt from state surveillance. Snowden, Assange, and Manning are also fighting on another, parallel, front, namely on the field of relations between the logic of the state and the call for democracy, which may prove to stand in fundamental contradiction to each other. Here, Snowden is not the main player. Manning's revelations and the actions undertaken by Assange, via WikiLeaks, occupy center stage.

In effect, the activities of Manning, Assange, and WikiLeaks take on a notion that often passes unquestioned: "state secrets." The challenge is to arouse people's sense that the existence of a secret sphere at the very core of state operations is problematic. Manning and Assange have posed the question of what might be called the "black box" of states. They refuse to accept the self-evident legitimacy of the idea that *not everything* should be transparent within the state—that is, the fact that a hidden sphere exists where information circulates and decisions are made without citizens ever knowing as much. In particular, this concern involves matters of diplomacy, the secret services, and military or industrial strategy.

The significance—and the grandeur—of WikiLeaks stems from its radical political and theoretical approach, the way it approaches the problematic relations between secrecy, freedom of information, and democratic transparency. Assange's analysis is based, first and foremost, on the idea that the category of "secret"—that is, the right arrogated by states to withdraw information from public circulation—constitutes a measure that enables governmental agencies to commit criminal actions, or private parties to perform illegal acts that the state knows about but prefers to keep from being brought to general attention. "Leaking" such information represents a democratic necessity in any constitutional state that invokes the principle of equality before the law. Thus, Assange declares in an interview:

> One should now picture the state as a kind of box where some information goes in and other information comes out. Inside, certain data is carefully hidden; it likely concerns abuses of power, acts of injustice, and instances of corruption. And if citizens want to monitor their governments democratically, they have to know what's in the box. In other words, the box of the state should basically be transparent.[3]

Assange's analysis is both important and innovative because it goes beyond reflection on illegal state activities and the revelation of the failures that administrations try to hide. It is more radical—and, for the same reason, more beautiful—because it bears on *the idea of state secrecy itself*.

In effect, even democratic states harbor the innate tendency to establish, at their very core, a sphere that is nondemocratic, nonpublic, and neither supervised nor supervisable. Statesmen are convinced—as are citizens, often—that such an arrangement is necessary, that it is imperative for there to be spheres of action, negotiation, and decision where secrecy and a hermetic principle prevail: reasons of state, diplomacy, and bargaining all require discretion; by definition, interventions by the secret services and military strategies may not be made public; and so on.

This belief, firmly anchored in the practices (habitus) of men and women in the state apparatus, is what Assange intends to deconstruct; very actively, he sets to work taking apart the nondemocratic sphere within democratic states. As such, his engagement entails redefining the notion of the state, how connections between citizens and the administration are conceived, as well as the modes by which international relations operate.

For Assange, the notion of a "state secret" is, at bottom, an illusion and a snare. It would have us believe that certain kinds of information are not accessible to anyone. Yet all secrets circulate in some fashion and are shared; consequently, what is called "secret" therefore amounts in fact to public information, but only for a public defined by institutional, state, or arbitrary borders (based on collaboration between agencies, hearsay, and so on). A state secret is information that is public yet hidden—public information within a restricted group, but blocked to outsiders. Thus, the notion serves above all to *erect borders within the field of legitimate access to information.*[4]

The orchestration of this restricted flow of information functions as a mechanism of dispossession. It engineers an imbalance between rulers and ruled; inasmuch as state logic operates independently of the public, it is incompatible with the very idea of democracy. The state apparatus commands knowledge that is structurally denied to the public—or, more precisely, it organizes the public's ignorance of the same. The foundations of and motivations for political decisions thereby escape democratic supervision. Privatizing information deprives the ruled of the ability to monitor those who rule them. It operates as a principle of subjugation that holds the people in a condition of minority and heteronomy.

To be sure, it is difficult to imagine the form that a perfectly transparent state—one without secrets, a black box, dissimulation, and so on—would assume. We are so accustomed to associating "state" and "secret" that transparency in the sphere of politics and decision making strikes us as an impossibility. But conversely, one might consider transparency as a *self-evident* condition for democratic rule in the first place. What is more, it is curious—and the matter calls for reflection—that we so readily concede that establishing democratic rule requires maintaining a nondemocratic sphere—as if the democratic promise necessarily had to remain incompletely realized, continuously hindered.

WikiLeaks rises up against the assumption that a democratic state should accept nondemocratic spheres, outside the law, where arbitrary decisions reign. The organization, founded in 2006, has taken as its slogan: "Privacy for the weak, transparency for the powerful." In so doing, it seeks to provide a secure framework where citizens may deposit information—in other words, reveal to the public what ordinarily would remain hidden. WikiLeaks guarantees anonymity to its contributors and means to create an interface among whistle-blowers, journalists, and the public.[5] Encouraging leaks is meant to help make states transparent. It is worth mentioning that certain theorists and activists within this dynamic entity understand the mere existence of WikiLeaks as an apparatus to promote morality in government (thereby taking up Foucault's critical account of the panopticon as a system for disciplining the bodies and minds of those potentially subjected to its surveillance and control, and transforming it into a positive phenomenon).

Of the leaks that the organization has diffused, those that have had the most resonance are the ones that simultaneously involved state secrets and criminal activity on the part of authorities. They occurred in 2010–2011, thanks to actions taken by Chelsea Manning, then a military analyst. Manning is known for having transmitted classified documents to WikiLeaks. Her revelations, of considerable dimension and import, exposed illegal actions committed by the American army. The most famous leak is the video "Collateral Murder," showing an aerial raid on Baghdad that took place 12 July 2007, in the course of which an American helicopter opened fire on a group of civilians—including two reporters from Reuters. At least eighteen people were killed. Likewise, Manning stands behind the disclosure, to the world press, of the "cables" that made an immense portion of American diplomatic activity available to the public. In 2010, WikiLeaks began publishing what eventually amounted to more than two hundred thousand telegrams; when broadcast through media outlets, they brought general attention to the subterranean state activity normally called "diplomacy" or "international relations": hidden negotiations, competition for influence, rumor-mongering, strategic lies, information concealed even from allies, and so on.

Radicalizing the Call for Democracy

Whether revelations bear on illegal activities by state agencies or concern activities that are legal but secret, it is clearly a matter of using the Internet and the "technique" of leaks to radicalize the call for democracy: the law should apply everywhere, for rulers and ruled alike; citizens should be able to fully monitor their governments. The view that the state may legitimately make decisions and act covertly counts as fundamentally antidemocratic—and potentially authoritarian. Snowden expressed this conviction when discussing the espionage programs he had revealed:

> The secret continuance of these progams represents a far greater danger than their disclosure. . . . [P]rograms that are implemented in secret, out of public oversight, lack . . . legitimacy, and that's a problem. It also represents a dangerous normalization of "governing in the dark," where decisions with enormous public impact occur without any public input.[6]

Before proceeding, it should be stressed that the vehement hostility toward WikiLeaks demonstrated by states and the quasi-hysterical reaction on the part of rulers may be largely explained by the narcissistic wound that the organization's activities inflict on the men and women who hold state power. Indeed, it is difficult to measure just how much the latter derive enjoyment from having access to information denied to the public (which is hereby constituted as an ignorant mass): an entire vision of oneself as a privileged, rational being—in touch with a rarefied realm from which ordinary citizens are excluded—structures the self-image of those belonging to the apparatus of government. This is one of the strongest symbolic remunerations that the state offers to those who serve it. The activities of Wikileaks tear down such class privilege. The whole doctrine animating the site aims to strip members of the state of what is perhaps their most important social asset: the ability to view others as ignorant. For them, all that happens here amounts to intolerable aggression—hence the violence of their reactions. Fundamentally, the matter differs little from bourgeois reactions to political actors who encourage popular access to museums and classical music concerts, that is, spaces that were once symbolically reserved for the bourgeoisie. Losing hold of exclusive access to rare goods is one of the phenomena of social life that occasions the most violent reactions.

Abolishing all the obscurity built into state operations; making the government's functions, decisions, and motivations for those decisions transparent; and doing away with the very idea of state secrecy: these are the axes of the struggles that have emerged in the wake of actions undertaken by Snowden, Assange, and Manning.

Needless to say, nuances, differences, and perhaps even points of opposition exist between Snowden, Assange, and Manning; more generally, the same holds for all who occupy this space of reflection and militant activism. For example, Snowden's declarations occasionally suggest that he considers the essential problem as stemming from the fact that surveillance programs have been set up without public monitoring: the decision should have been the citizens' to make. Assange, in contrast, questions the legitimacy of such programs in the first place.

That said, and whatever differences there may be, it is still possible to discern a guiding principle that unites all of these efforts. It is a matter of renewing—and perhaps radicalizing—the call for democracy in the Internet age. Snowden, Assange, and Manning are reactivating the political and legal struggles against arbitrary state power that have been playing out since the nineteenth century. The questions they pose about private life and surveillance, illegal acts committed by authorities, and state secrets are fed by a democratic ambition. The point is, on the one hand, to protect the personal realm against state intrusion and, on the other, to extend the supervision exercised by the ruled over those who rule—in defiance of the fact that the political field increasingly has come to operate in secret, by taking the liberty to make decisions hidden from citizens.

CHAPTER 2

DISMANTLING THE LAW

IN POSING THE QUESTION of how to defend civil liberties—and, more generally, in underscoring the need to maintain the legal order and foundations of a liberal constitution against increasingly pronounced governmental tendencies to dismantle its very structure—Snowden, Assange, and Manning stand at the heart of any number of pressing contemporary issues. Their battles are part of the reflections that have arisen, on an international scale, from the transformations in juridico-political frameworks following the attacks of 11 September 2001. The "War on Terror" and the idea of "protecting national security" have rendered constitutional frameworks increasingly fragile. NSA spying programs and the preservation of "state secrets" belong to an array of phenomena that include the camp at Guantánamo Bay, secret CIA bases, and the arrest and detention—without charges—of individuals the Patriot Act has qualified as "enemy combatants." Such realities manifest a logic that is only growing in force: the tendency of states to create an extralegal sphere and multiply the mechanisms for making exceptions.

Along these lines, Giorgio Agamben has analyzed the anti-terrorist legislation enacted in the United States after September 11 along with related operations that adjourn regular law or diminish legal safeguards. Among other matters, he discusses how the law includes its own suspension in

> the "military order" issued by the president of the United States on November 13, 2001, which authorized the "indefinite detention" and trial by "military commissions" . . . of noncitizens suspected of involvement in terrorist activities. . . .
>
> What is new about President Bush's order is that it radically erases any legal status of the individual, thus producing a legally unnamable and unclassifiable being. Not only do the Taliban captured in Afghanistan not enjoy the status of POWs as defined by the Geneva Convention, they do not even have the status of persons charged with a crime according to American law. Neither prisoners nor persons accused, but simply "detainees," they are the object of a pure de facto rule, of a detention that is indefinite not only in the temporal sense but in its very nature as well, since it is entirely removed from the law and from judicial oversight.[1]

It follows that the political scene of our day is characterized by states working to weaken the frameworks that protect our lives from arbitrary exercises of power. Governments are allowing themselves to suspend safeguards and thereby creating individuals deprived of rights—if not stripped of nationality. This process is undoing the efficacy of the rules at the very foundation of liberal constitutions.

Likewise, Judith Butler has drawn attention to how states deprive subjects of legal guarantees:

> Doubtless, one reason for the rise of interest in Carl Schmitt, perhaps also in Giorgio Agamben's work on this topic, has

been the idea that constitutions carry within them the rights of the sovereign to suspend constitutional protections. This runs counter to certain ways of telling the story about the rise of democratic constitutionalism in which sovereignty is overcome through contractarian forms of parliamentary government. In particular, Agamben's reading of the "state of exception" clearly resonates with the operation of power that we have seen in the suspension of constitutional rights to trial and the imprisonment of populations in the name of national security.[2]

Butler develops this analysis further in *Precarious Life*, devoting a chapter to the question of "indefinite detention."[3] For her, the conditions of detention at Guantánamo—that is, the possibility of indefinite imprisonment determined by executive fiat without any judicial oversight (and therefore with no chance for appeal, because the detainee has not been formally accused)—represent a legal innovation whose implications have yet to be appreciated in full. This arrangement should provide the point of departure for understanding how state power, sovereignty, and governmentality are now in the course of changing.

States—and chief among them, the United States—are instrumentalizing the idea of a war on terror and invoking the existence of dangerous individuals who threaten national security in order to augment the sovereign nature of their exercise of power. Detainees at Guantánamo (they are not called "prisoners" because they might otherwise appeal to the rights afforded to ordinary prisoners) are not subject to any judiciary instance. Instead, the executive oversees how their fate is regulated: the administration decides whether they will stand trial or not; even in the event of acquittal, it reserves the right not to liberate detainees if it still considers them dangerous. As such, Guantánamo represents a highly charged site in the landscape of contemporary democracy because the law is not binding here: executive power has detached itself from the constitutional limitations that are supposed to frame it, and it no longer recognizes the authority of the courts. The state has granted itself the option not to heed judicial power. Today's economy of power is shaped by the fact that the state is enlisting strategic imperatives in order to suspend the law, adjourn its application, and deprive certain individuals of the protections it affords.

The analysis offered here aims to draw out transformations that bear on the present, the place we occupy within it, and, especially, the nature of the relations that tie us to the state and constitute us as subjects. The goal is to understand how a new economy of power is being set in place that creates a new image of legal subjecthood and citizenship. The discussion highlights the fact that we are witnessing a reworking of the function of sovereignty, specifically in its relation to law. According to traditional political theory, sovereign power is defined in terms of the law—as an instance deriving its authority from a set of statutes and from their applications by the ways that the police and justice systems apply them. But today, sovereignty has begun operating differently. It is no longer manifest in the application of the law. Instead, it achieves expression when the latter is suspended. The state affirms its sovereignty by declaring its right not to obey the law. Judith Butler puts it like this: it is not so much the sovereign who suspends the law; it is the act of suspending the law that creates the sovereign nature of state power.[4]

It is within this general context, this contemporary space of questions and concerns, that the revelations of Snowden, Assange, and Manning operate. Issues of privacy, surveillance, and state secrecy constitute one of the battlefields where the struggle to defend both individual rights and lofty legal principles from state incursions is unfolding. Noam Chomsky has made this diagnosis in explicit terms: White House lawyers are in the process of demolishing our civil liberties. Snowden, Assange, and Manning have alerted the public to the progressive dislocation of legal frameworks, and their acts of insurgency should encourage collective mobilization to call states back to the order established by the law and the constitution.[5]

CHAPTER 3

POLITICS, SOVEREIGNTY, EXCEPTION

JUDITH BUTLER'S, GIORGIO AGAMBEN'S, AND NOAM CHOMSKY'S analyses of the economy of power and sovereignty bear on the particular context of the course states have taken since 11 September 2001. However, their interest is not restricted to this historical situation alone. Quite the opposite: these analyses belong to a larger project that seeks to redefine the relationship between theoretical reflection and the problems of law, democracy, and the state. As such, they exemplify how the notions of law and of citizenship are proving problematic in our times.

I would like to reconstruct the language these authors share to show how it orients our understanding of law and of rights, that is, of how we conceive of ourselves in relation to the state. Following that, I will seek to explain how the figures of Snowden, Assange, and Manning make it possible to reformulate the idiom of contemporary critical philosophy. In other words: if (along with almost everyone else, including the actors themselves) we understand their actions as part of the traditional form of the general struggle to defend liberty and rights, their specificity vanishes: we lose sight of the singularity of the questions they have posed, in a concrete manner, concerning the state, the law, and the nation—in other words, the ways in which they enable us to think differently about both the mechanisms at play and our potential to free ourselves from them.

Incompleteness

Critical theory is always anchored in the present. The formulas it presents bear traces of its moment of genesis, and those traces should not be seen as faults or symptoms of an incompletely developed theory. On the contrary, they constitute the palpable manifestation of an essential intention: to link conceptual activity to the question posed by the present and to seek out murky zones within it as sites from which one may fashion instruments for thinking differently and articulating new modes of observation.

To a large extent, the course that much of contemporary theory has steered with regard to the law and the state may be explained by the changes in our political and historical circumstances, which have only become more pronounced since the beginning of this century. These transformations have influenced critical analysis and the way in which it calls the law into question—that is, the way it identifies aspects of the legal-political order that prove problematic. To be sure, the processes that have dislocated laws and rights and caused extralegal spaces to proliferate under the pretext of the "War on Terror" have characterized movements that have grown in intensity since 11 September 2001. But at the same time, they have provided the point of departure for the development of a new analysis of law and rights in general, a new method for understanding their positivity and identifying their limitations. These modifications have drawn attention to the phenomena of extralegality and to the *exception*: that which escapes the law within the law itself. Contemporary critical theory has reclaimed these phenomena and made them the focus of its investigation.

Thus, the critique of the state and of sovereignty is centered on the notion of incompleteness. At the heart of its analysis stands the idea that the legal order is consubstantial with a sphere of extra-legality. Counter to what we might think, extralegality (i.e., the arbitrary exercise of power or unregulated relationships of power) does not occupy a position standing to one side of the law, as something merely awaiting integration into its regulatory operations; nor is it simply the remnant of an earlier legal state that has not yet been entirely uprooted. Instead, it is involved in the production of justice and law, a site inscribed within—and instituted by—justice and the law: extralegality represents a situation of power called for and constructed by the logic of legality itself. The fact that the legal systems of liberal democracies are subject to critique is rooted in the fact that they exhibit gaps at every juncture. The state order is constantly effecting operations of dispossession, discrimination, and exclusion. These are the situations that provide the focus for the critique, whose analysis takes them as its point of departure.

The Exception

The flip side of the law, which is built into the law itself, takes the form, in Agamben's parlance, of the "state of exception." In *Homo Sacer* and *State of Exception*, he sets out to show how liberal democracies are predicated on a kind of paradoxical sovereignty: at the discretion of the sovereign, rights may be rightfully suspended—the law may legally be rendered inoperative. The traditional narrative holds that political power derives its legitimacy from the fact that it rests on a set of laws, norms, and constitutional rules. But as Agamben emphasizes, the legal structure framing sovereign power never applies completely. It recognizes that exceptions exist. The sovereign is defined by a singular capacity, that of freeing him- or herself from the law. The sovereign's exceptional status enables him or her to determine what constitutes an exception and, in turn, to appeal to this exception in order to suspend the legal order or to create situations that it does not cover, where it does not apply. Guantánamo is an example of this. The sovereign has the ability to invoke certain imperatives in order to cast off the legal restraints that otherwise hold and to promulgate decrees that have the force of law without the source of their legality being identifiable, because the ordinary legal frameworks have been suspended. The sovereign commands the right to determine a state of exception: to establish the possibility, in the name of the protection and self-preservation of the political and social body, for the law no longer to hold at any given moment.

According to Agamben, this ambivalence defines the architecture of liberalism: the government reserves the right to set itself outside the legal order—to escape the law. What is more, the decision to declare a state of emergency (that is, legitimate motives for doing so) can never, by definition, be legally encoded—after all, such a declaration is supposed to respond to exceptional and unforeseeable circumstances. Accordingly, the legal order does not establish a system of law in opposition to some preexisting state of anomie. It is incomplete. It is itself structured by an internal fragility and an "anomic zone." The law does not guarantee a set of protections against the arbitrariness of the sovereign, because the sovereign can disregard them at will.

The possibility of the state of exception is at the very heart of the architecture of political power. By virtue of this fact, it harbors the ruin of the construction upon which the Western legal system has been erected: rights, the law, and the state do not represent the triumph of regulated order over chaos because they are structurally based on, and shot through with, situations of indeterminacy, undecidability, and arbitrary discretion—which, in a way, empties them of their meaning.[1] This is so much the case that it begins to blur the difference between liberal democracies and other political regimes. Even in liberal democracies, the sovereign maintains the ability to act willfully, outside the law—that is, to cast off the constraints of legality and create situations where the law does not apply; this may take a positive form, such as granting pardons,[2] or a negative form, for example when foreigners seeking refugee status are detained in special waiting areas in international airports.[3] In other words, the very border between absolutism and democracy, between a police state and a state founded on the rule of law, grows murky, if it is not erased altogether.[4]

Statelessness

The analysis Agamben proposes, then, starts by taking into account realities that lie outside legality—conditions or processes that negate the regular order of rights and the law. The legal-political order admits criticism because it harbors instances of exception, emergency, and necessity that dismantle it from within and undermine its architecture and pretensions.

Judith Butler's writings on the nation-state, citizenship, and sovereignty also illustrate how this mode of investigation underlies many important approaches to politics. *Parting Ways: Jewishness and the Critique of Zionism* offers a critical assessment of such mechanisms, the ways in which they function, and their effects. Indeed, it is striking how Butler places the category of "dispossession" at the center of her analysis. Her critique of the legal order takes up the procedures of exclusion at work in legal operations—in other words, it explores how legality produces extralegality or, more specifically, situations in which individuals, groups, and/or minorities are stripped of legal protections. The critique of the nation-state, as a form of political organization, starts by focusing on the category that encompasses exiles, the stateless, and refugees: "the conditions of the stateless and the refugee [are] crucial to my understanding of human rights and of the critique of the nation-state, imprisonment and detention, torture and its ratification by law or policy."[5]

According to Butler, the construction of nation-states—that is, legally constituted states—always entails the exclusion of populations outside of the nation-state. Inasmuch as it is haunted by a certain ideology of the nation or of its national identity, every nation-state has the innate propensity to create individuals who are expelled because they do not match the idea, the unity, and/or the definition of the nation, and therefore also to deprive them of the legal protections that states are supposed to afford; these are the refugees, exiles, and the stateless. Butler takes up and elaborates on Hannah Arendt's position in order to show how the history of nation-states, as it has evolved since the nineteenth century, cannot be separated from experiences of dispossession, expulsion, and internment. If the problem of statelessness and refugees recurred throughout the twentieth century, this is because the period witnessed the triumph of the nation-state as a form. As Butler observes, Arendt insists

> that one has to think about this problem of refugees and the stateless as a repeated problem attached to states that are formed on the model of the nation-state. One might well ask what states are like that are not the same as nation-states, whether nation-states can exist without producing the horrendous consequence of massive numbers of stateless minorities, whether the problem is structural or historical, or both.[6]

Here again, the critique of law and rights is linked to the exclusions it produces. What is problematic about nation-states is rooted in the fact that their formation entails, by its nature, a mass of stateless minorities. To be sure, the constitution of the nation-state grants certain individuals the status of citizen. However, this operation of inclusion is never total. It is only ever partial—and it has a dark side. Inclusion entails operations excluding those who are not recognized as members of the nation: accordingly, they wind up being thrown into a situation where they have no nationality and become subject to violent and arbitrary powers (incarceration, deportation, and so on).

The categories of "exception" and "statelessness" occupy analogous positions. One could even say that the two terms refer to the same phenomenon, but viewed from different perspectives. In either case, the same diagnosis holds: *laws and rights are intrinsically tied to a sphere outside the law.* In the first instance, this extralegal realm comes into focus from within the sphere of justice and law (as the exception); in the second case, the extralegality occurs outside the sphere of justice and law (when people are deprived of rights). The key point is that the underlying structure is identical: it is from the point of view of extralegality that the law is examined. The critique starts from what has been shut out, in order to question what has been admitted and the principle of inclusion; it fastens on the exterior in order to examine the interior. The condition of statelessness opens the way for critiquing the nation-state; analyzing the exception exposes the invisible logic, indeed the impossibility, of the rule of justice and law.

PART II

DEFYING THE LAW

THE CONTEMPORARY CRITIQUE of law, justice, and politics is both subtle
and radical. The states of exclusion, inequality, discrimination, and
dispossession at the heart of the critique do not represent "flaws" or
"shortcomings" of the legal order. The point is not to conceptualize
them as matters of "dysfunction" that could be remedied by extend-
ing, completing, or systematizing legal logic as it stands. On the contrary, zones of extralegality and the operations that initiate them are
deemed to be consubstantial with the legal order: they result from its
intrinsic logic and modes of operation. Consequently, the critique of
law and rights proposed here calls for redefining the juridico-political
system such as we know it. The task is not to correct the system, nor
is it a matter of remaining within the horizon of liberal constitutions and finding ways to fulfill their promises by minimizing inad-
equacies and lacunae. Critique means refusing to ratify the order as
it stands. It means showing that establishing a political regime that
would not produce statelessness and refugees—or, for that matter,
a gray area of undecidability ("exception")—requires us to imagine
a new legal apparatus. Judith Butler, for instance, offers reflections

on the federation as an alternative form of political organization to
the nation-state.

But the radicalism of such analyses cannot conceal the fact that,
implicitly, a certain ratification of the legal order still remains at work.
These approaches are conditioned by and based on an underlying
adherence to the legal order. After all, the arguments always seek to
valorize the constitutional state and the rule of law as protective and
positive frameworks, while all that falls outside them is presented in a
negative light. The problematic aspect of the law lies in the exception,
which frustrates and undoes the due functioning of legal norms; the
problematic feature of the nation-state concerns the exclusion and
dispossession that it causes: the creation of stateless groups and refugees. In short, in this kind of analytical language, the critique of the
legal order concentrates on internal or external gaps, on moments
where it falls apart, on areas from which it withdraws, and so on.

What We Are

But what goes completely missing here, it seems to me, is the critique
of the law in its positive sense. That is why it strikes me as both possible and necessary to radicalize our contemporary critique in order
to interrogate the very categories of "legal order" and "politics." The
goal is not to focus on what is excluded or on situations where the
law finds no application, but to work out what the law itself actually
is—its nature and the definition of what it includes. The task, then,
is to make not statelessness, but citizenship, the object—not the state
of exception so much as the standard operations of the state founded
on the rule of law.

I would like to propose a contribution to the critique of legal
operations and the political order that focuses on the notions of
citizen, state, law, and the like. I submit that inasmuch as it does
not ask about these apparatuses—and indeed, it even holds them up
as points of reference in contradistinction to which the "negative"

then is conceived—contemporary critique acts as if they concerned unproblematic, transparent categories that do not require examination, as if they were not shot through with the operations of power at every level. But what is needed is the very opposite: to demonstrate the problematic nature of being a legal subject, what it means to be subject to the order of law, the implications of citizenship, and the modes of subjectification these frames impose. If we want to understand what we are—the operations of power that apply to us, the regulations that define and determine what we can be—we need a theory that will permit us to grasp what it means to be a legal subject, the violence to which we stand exposed inasmuch as we are citizens, members of a state, and subjects of the law. What are the operations at work when we are included in the legal order, when we live in a democratic regime and *belong* to a nation?

Needless to say, asking questions of this sort does not mean equating the positions occupied by citizens and stateless persons, nor does it mean equating arbitrary and regular modes of government. The critique of legality I am advancing does not seek to neutralize differences. The task of integral, radical critique does not entail situating rights and laws on the same register as what lies outside them. In undertaking a critique of the constitutional state and of citizenship understood in positive terms, I do not wish to claim that the constitutional state and citizenship harbor as many instances of violence, as many instances of limitation, as do a police state or the condition of exile—nor do I claim that circumstances prove equally problematic in either case. I certainly agree that rights, the law, and the constitution afford protections; when they are not extended to all, or come to be suspended, this amounts to dispossession. At the same time, however, this view should not lead one to ratify the values of the legal order, nor should it prevent one from conducting a critical investigation of the type of subjectivity that follows from the fact of being inscribed in a state. Otherwise, our critique will effectively maintain a certain kind of statism in our thinking, that is, ratify the logic of legality and citizenship. The project of critiquing the state, the legal order, and political frameworks ought to be preserved and affirmed: it should enable us to bring into the open the operations of power and forms of violence that work, in hidden fashion, through these apparatuses; doing so will give us the means to confront these forms of organization with the demands of democracy and liberty in order to open up a new political horizon, one that is more emancipatory and affords greater protections.[1]

Specifically, the thesis I wish to advance is that the actions and lives of Snowden, Assange, and Manning interrogate, in their very form and mode of engagement, the order of legality and the architecture of liberal democracies. In other words, the broad-scale struggles that have unfolded around them, which they exemplify in their persons, amount to something more than the desire to call states back to the rule of law and constitutional norms. That view fastens on just one aspect of what is at stake, for it applies the analytical scheme of the prevailing critique of power and sovereignty and places these figures on a predetermined field of battle; in so doing, it prevents us from seeing what is new, singular, and unprecedented here.[2]

Doing justice to what Snowden, Assange, and Manning have undertaken, to who and what they are, requires us not to focus exclusively on the stakes of what they are protesting or the questions this raises. We must also examine their modes of protest: in the ways they revolt, the manner in which they have constituted themselves as subjects engaged in struggle, they have set up, in practical terms, a new relationship to legality, the state, and dissidence. Significantly, they have not laid claim to existing forms of revolt, nor are they content to present new items of contention on the preestablished stage of public engagement. Instead, their attack takes aim at the political stage itself. They call into question the frameworks of politics, the prescribed forms of activism and expression—and, in so doing, contest the mechanism of democratic politics as we know it, as it is imposed on us. As we know, it is always much more subversive to question the mechanisms themselves than to make statements, even very radical ones, within recognized, institutionalized settings. Snowden, Assange, and Manning do not simply point out the failures of democracies and show us processes for "dismantling" ordinary legal rules. They embody a *challenge to the law itself.* They ask what is still nondemocratic within the values and ideals that we traditionally acknowledge to be the symbols of democracy.

A New Political Arena

And yet, when reference is made to the actions of Snowden, Assange, and Manning—as well as to the activities of those who have followed in their wake (whistle-blowers, hackers, Anonymous, and so on)—the term one hears the most often, the phrase that seems most fitting at first, is a classic category: "civil disobedience." To be sure, Snowden, Assange, and Manning have performed illegal acts: they downloaded secret documents, obtained information without authorization, made classified reports public, and so forth. But the illegality of these actions, I want to argue, is a matter of appearance: it certainly does not stand in the way of their legitimacy, since the objective was to denounce illegal actions on the part of the state (unauthorized surveillance, illicit programs, and actions contrary to legal rules).

As Noam Chomsky declared when debating the notion of justice with Michel Foucault,[3] the practice of civil disobedience rests on a simple axiom: not granting the monopoly over what counts as legal or just to what conforms to the order of law at a given moment. It is possible for the state to be criminal. Accordingly, disobeying a law can represent a legal action. And further: if the state acts in a criminal manner, contrary to the constitution, it is the *duty* of citizens—not just morally but, above all, legally—to put a stop to it: "very often when I do something which the state regards as illegal, I regard it as legal: that is, I regard the state as criminal."[4] Chomsky provides the example of resistance and disobedience to the conduct of imperialist wars, citing the Vietnam War, in particular:

> there are interesting elements of international law, for example, embedded in the Nuremberg principles and the United Nations Charter, which permit, in fact, I believe, *require* the citizen to act against his own state in ways which the state will falsely regard as criminal. Nevertheless, he's acting legally, because international law also happens to prohibit the threat or use of force in international affairs, except under some very narrow circumstances, of which, for example, the war in Vietnam is not one. This means that in the particular case of the Vietnam War, which interests me most, the American state is acting in a criminal capacity. And the people have the right to stop criminals from committing murder. Just because the criminal happens to call your action illegal when you try to stop him, that doesn't mean it *is* illegal.[5]

Thus, interpreting the actions of Snowden, Assange, and Manning as civil disobedience amounts to inscribing them in the continuum of the great democratic struggles of the nineteenth and twentieth centuries—from the fight against slavery to the struggle for civil rights, from protests against the Vietnam War to movements for gay marriage or against genetically modified organisms (e.g., the *Faucheurs volontaires* in France).

Following this logic, these three militants—like many other political actors before them—have taken the liberty of disobeying in order to denounce and stop harmful, if not illegal, measures undertaken by the state. Clearly, this interpretation is perfectly coherent in terms of the ordinary perception that their actions occurred in reaction to threats bearing on our civil liberties: facing mounting measures that declared a state of exception or pursued illegal aims, they intervened to rouse the public and bring the state back to the rule of law. But I would like to challenge this interpretation. I do not believe that Snowden, Assange, and Manning can be viewed as falling within the tradition of civil disobedience. The category does not strike me as relevant in this context.

I interpret this classification as a rhetorical operation: because we don't have the words to name what is new, we fall back on older categories. This designation is also a matter of strategy: when new movements emerge, they are precarious and fragile by nature, and unsure of themselves. Thus, we tend to want to assign them some legitimacy by inscribing them alongside movements that already occupy an important symbolic place in our political imaginary.

I know full well that Snowden and Manning also use these same categories when speaking of themselves. I believe them to be mistaken, however, and I think that it is important to think about how and why they are mistaken about themselves. They are inventing new subjectivities without being aware of it.

Of course, what is at stake is more than a matter of "naming." Questions of definition do not hold much interest, either. The real stakes lie elsewhere. To analyze how the actions of Snowden, Assange, and Manning do not quite align with the principles of civil disobedience may seem like a secondary question—a technical problem or simply a matter of vocabulary. I believe, on the contrary, that it is a very important issue in reflecting critically on politics. I submit that the distance between the actions performed by Snowden, Assange, and Manning, on the one hand, and the forms that civil disobedience assumes, on the other, marks the critical site, the fault line, where the novelty of what is taking place through them can be discerned.

In fact, civil disobedience does not represent one mode of protest among others. On the contrary, this form of revolt goes as far as possible within what is permitted within the bounds authorized by liberal democracy as we know it.[6] Of all options available for voicing dissent—for denouncing a law, a ruling, and so on—it stands as the most forceful gesture, one that is often used only as a last resort. Indeed, in a sense, one could even say that it represents the most radically democratic practice of all, inasmuch as it makes use of the categories of law, citizenship, constitution, and so on in the most seditious and anti-establishment manner possible.[7]

And so, analyzing how and why Snowden, Assange, and Manning adopted positions out of step with this mechanism does not merely enable us to reflect on the nature of civil disobedience and its blind spots and limitations—or perhaps even on its conservative features (which, as we shall see, should inspire us to proceed with caution in evaluating the multiplying number of movements that lay claim to it). Such an analysis also opens the way for exploring a mode of political subjectification that eludes prescribed and preestablished forms—and thus for questioning the effects of power, censorship, and violence that these instituted forms entail. How do the notions of citizenship, the law, the state, and the public sphere work? What paths might be taken by subjectivity once it has been released from the existing codes of expression in liberal democracies? What effects would this produce?

Civil Disobedience

The classic work for understanding the nature of civil disobedience and what it reveals about the subjectivity of those who practice it— that is, their relationship to the law and the state—is undoubtedly John Rawls's *Theory of Justice.* Here, Rawls reflects at length on how to define, and then justify, civil disobedience. He restricts his discussion to the framework of established democratic authority because he considers that the problem of the legitimacy, to say nothing of the legality, of dissidence only arises under governments where the process of formulating laws is democratic; under authoritarian or dictatorial regimes, the legitimacy of opposition is manifest. (It is important to note that Rawls's analyses have been adopted by actual movements of civil disobedience, which invoke his theory and see themselves in it, such that they may be taken to express the values underlying this approach.)

Rawls defines civil disobedience as "a public, nonviolent, conscientious yet political act contrary to law usually done with the aim of bringing about a change in the law or policies of the government."[8] As such, civil disobedience constitutes, first, a politics of interpellation and public mobilization: it appeals to the sense of justice—the sound, democratic sense of the majority and government—in order to obtain a reform of state practices.

> In justifying civil disobedience one does not appeal to principles of personal morality or to religious doctrines, though these may coincide with and support one's claims. . . . Instead one invokes the commonly shared conception of justice that underlies the political order. It is assumed that in a reasonably just democratic regime there is a public conception of justice by reference to which citizens regulate their political affairs and interpret the constitution. The persistent and deliberate violation of the basic principles of this conception over any extended period of time, especially the infringement of the fundamental equal liberties, invites either submission or resistance.[9]

Therefore, even when a minority decides to employ this method of protest, mobilization always occurs in the name of majoritarian values—or, more accurately, in the name of values that count as those of society, so-called shared values (and this notion of shared values seems very problematic to me):

> Civil disobedience is a political act not only in the sense that it
> is addressed to the majority that holds political power, but also

because it is an act guided and justified by political principles, that is, by the principles of justice which regulate the constitution and social institutions generally.[10]

Publicness

Despite its apparently singular and radical character, civil disobedience is continuous with the most traditional democratic forms. Its first characteristic is to be public. The subject or the collective that disobeys is supposed to disobey publicly, in plain sight, and explicitly:

> Civil disobedience is a public act. Not only is it addressed to public principles, it is done in public. It is engaged in openly with fair notice; it is not covert or secretive. One may compare it to public speech, and being a form of address, an expression of profound and conscientious political conviction, it takes place in the public forum.[11]

The very logic of civil disobedience calls for this public quality, which is inscribed as a necessity in the meaning and function of such an action. Above all, disobeying aims to appeal to opinion, to intervene in political deliberation. In publicly affirming that I am disobeying a law I consider illegitimate, I am addressing others—or, to put it somewhat differently, I mean to call on my society to live up to its principles and denounce instances where the state seems to betray the foundations of its existence. As such, civil disobedience means confronting society with itself, its ideals of justice, so that it will conform with what it claims to be.

Disobedience—defying the forces of order—would appear to mean defying the state itself. In reality, however, it is simply a mobilization destined to accommodate or reform it. Civil disobedience is not a practice that contests the legal order. On the contrary, it reinvokes the law. Protestors deviate from what counts as legal at a given moment in the name of the "values" of democratic society. This form of protest takes place in the name of the law. One might even say that dissidents seek to be even more legalistic than the state.

For this same reason, we should note, civil disobedience does not represent an inventive practice—a means for political innovation to take place. To the extent that civil disobedience unfolds in the name of "social values"—if, in fact, this expression has any meaning at all (and herein lies the whole problem)—to the extent that civil disobedience occurs in the name of the "constitution," it sets out to ratify these same values and takes these norms as given, once and for all. In other words, it means assuming a position that precludes fashioning new ones.

Thus, it is clear, the person who practices civil disobedience, who engages in struggle of this kind, is not subjectifying him- or herself as a seditious being, as one adhering to values approaching anarchism or standing at odds with the constitutional state and its laws. On the contrary, the subject of civil disobedience is a subject of the state through and through. He or she acts in the name of the law and acknowledges his or her inscription in the legal system. At the same time, however, it is from this same position that he or she derives the requirement to disobey a given law publicly, inasmuch as it proves manifestly incompatible with the values of justice.

Responsibility

Such recognition of the law, which precedes and conditions the act of civil disobedience, is evident in the fact that the subjectivity of those who disobey entails responsibility for the acts performed and a willingness to answer for them. As a matter of course, the act of disobedience provokes a repressive response from the state and opens the risk of punishment. Subjects who engage in civil disobedience do not seek to escape sanction. They recognize its legitimacy and allow themselves to be punished. Engaging in civil disobedience means considering oneself subject to punishment. Disobeying, being summoned before the law, and getting punished represent a *typical* series of steps. Indeed, it is in this fashion that the legalism of movements and, by the same token, their sincerity come into view:

> Civil disobedience is nonviolent for another reason. It expresses disobedience to law within the limits of fidelity to law, although it is at the outer edge thereof. The law is broken, but fidelity to law is expressed by the public and nonviolent nature of the act, by the willingness to accept the legal consequences of one's conduct. This fidelity to law helps to establish to the majority that the act is indeed politically conscientious and sincere, and that it is intended to address the public's sense of justice.[12]

Accepting punishment represents part of a system; it goes along with the nonviolent character of civil disobedience. This acceptance and nonviolence are two sides of one and the same tactic, which aims to demonstrate the *violence* of the law. Peacefully disobeying, allowing oneself to be arrested, being punished: this whole sequence gives rise to a dramaturgy whereby nonviolence belongs to those protesting while repression and the use of force are features of the state. By setting up an opposition between the pacifism of the protesters and the state's repressive violence, this mise-en-scène seeks to appeal to public opinion and raise awareness of the authorities' injustice so that further mobilization will occur in order to change the law.

Submitting oneself to repressive measures, and even calling for one's own punishment, are hallmarks of the gesture of civil disobedience. This much is evident in the foundational work by Henry David Thoreau that first articulated the practice. In *Civil Disobedience*, Thoreau explains how his objection to the Mexican-American War and his opposition to slavery in the states of the American South led him to disobey—specifically, by refusing to pay taxes. Thoreau's text is complex and rich in reflection; as we will see, it holds many other implications, too. What merits emphasis in the context at hand is Thoreau's complete awareness that civil disobedience is inscribed within the game of penalty. He knows that in disobeying publicly, he is calling for punishment and will end up in prison. This, however, is precisely what he wants: he *should* land in jail. Thoreau likes jail, and he sings its praises. When it imprisons him, the state will openly display its injustice:

> Under a government which imprisons unjustly, the true place for a just man is also a prison. The proper place today, the only place which Massachusetts has provided for her freer and less despondent spirits, is in her prisons, to be put out and locked out of the state by her own act, as they have already put themselves out by their principles. It is there that the fugitive slave, and the Mexican prisoner on parole, and the Indian come to plead the wrongs of his race should find them; on that separate but more free and honorable ground, where the state places those who are not with her, but against her—the only house in a slave state in which a free man can abide with honor.[13]

Another Way

Civil disobedience is an extreme case: here, the art of revolt brings into play, in the most radical fashion, the categories underlying the architecture of liberal democracies. Therefore, civil disobedience can be used as a kind of enlarging mirror with which to reflect on our political unconscious, traditional ways of thinking, and the definitions we give to the categories of citizen, subject, and so on. The practice of civil disobedience provides a way to identify the logic that determines democratic existence both in periods of "calm" and in conditions of protest—in other words, the form of subjectification that is also operative in the most established and regular instances of disagreement (petitions, demonstrations, strikes, and so forth).

The main point is that for an act of disobedience to assume political meaning—that is, to be perceived not simply as a criminal act but as a mode of civic intervention—it must be performed by someone who entertains a certain relation to the public space, the political community, and responsibility. The engaged subject assumes a position in the public sphere, occupies that space, adopts a visible stance, and simultaneously, by virtue of the same, makes a statement or carries out actions that entail obligations; potentially, she or he will have to answer, and assume responsibility, for them. In order to act as a citizen—to enter the sphere of democracy—the subject should be identifiable, responsible, and act openly. This mode of subjectification is what constitutes a legal subject, that is, a citizen.

But if this is so, then Snowden, Assange, and Manning—as well as others participating in movements along related lines—have sought to deploy another mode of action, which defies these constraints and this kind of subjectification.

Chelsea Manning, for instance, did not perform an act of *civil* disobedience—an open action she claimed publicly—when she exposed the illegal practices of the American army and the secret services. On the contrary, she acted in a hidden, anonymous manner—and was only identified as the source of the leaks because she was denounced. Manning acted *politically, but without advancing a public claim or adopting a public stance.* What is more, she shared the information on the WikiLeaks site, which encourages such practices and modes of intervention. WikiLeaks, as Assange conceives it, is meant to provide an encrypted space where nothing can be traced; here, it ought to be impossible to determine the personal identity of the "source" of documents.[14] The new struggles taking shape around WikiLeaks, Manning's gesture, or, of course, the activities of groups like Anonymous deploy a new way of conducting politics, which avoids the issue of appearing in public. These battles use methods that lay claim to the practice of anonymity and nonappearance.

To be sure, Snowden and Assange, for their part, are figures who occupy public space. They acknowledge their actions, and their names are known. At the same time, albeit in a different way, they have effected a break with traditional democratic structures: they are challenging and calling into question the notion of a responsible subject. Instead of answering for their actions by calling for, and accepting, punishment on the model of Thoreau, who allowed himself to be arrested and imprisoned, Snowden and Assange have adopted a solitary practice of exile. They did not peacefully and passively allow themselves to be arrested and submitted to judgment—nor did Manning, for that matter. Their politics involve flight. On the public stage, they openly acknowledge their actions, but, at the same time, they are unwilling to define themselves as subjects who accept repressive measures. They have instead assumed the stance of "irresponsible" subjects who refuse to appear to face charges. Snowden, for one, left for Hong Kong before he made his disclosures. He lived in hiding there before he was forced to seek refuge in Moscow, and he has sought asylum in dozens of countries. These are not the kind of political subjects who, to employ Rawls's words, bear "the legal consequences of [their] actions." These are parties who run away from the consequences—who reject them and do everything in their power to escape them.

Clearly, Snowden, Assange, and Manning did not all act in the same fashion, on the same terms, or use the same methods. And yet, through their actions, the political scene is being displaced and a new form of political engagement is emerging. Each one of them, in his or her own way and from his or her particular angle, has taken a position at a remove from the prescribed position of political subjectivity. As such, they invite us to repoliticize certain questions. The subject they prefigure does not constitute a responsible party acting publicly in the political sphere. Instead, this subject intervenes anonymously, from a concealed position, refusing to take on the law personally or to recognize his or her inscription in the order of the law.

Such modes of action possess a critical dimension. What, for instance, does it mean to act politically in an anonymous manner? Why does this strike us as a contradiction in terms? In what ways does this mode of self-constitution as a subject involved in struggle call into question how contemporary democracy connects with a certain idea of public space and collective expression? Indeed, in broader terms, what is at stake in the desire for anonymity that finds expression on the Internet—including realms beyond or outside of politics?

And what, in turn, does it mean to tie an art of revolt to the practice of exile, of taking flight—which, in this context, is associated with the refusal to stand and face charges? How should we understand the relationship between political action and migratory practice, seeking to change one's country of residence or even nationality? What political power does this practice hold, and to what extent does it represent a crisis of given, "spontaneous" relations between individuals and the law, the state, national belonging, and so on? What can these types of subjectification teach us about our habitual ways of thinking about and practicing politics—and even of conceiving of ourselves, our place in the world, and our relationship to others?

PART III

NEW POLITICAL SUBJECTS

CHAPTER 4

ANONYMITY, PUBLIC SPACE, AND DEMOCRACY

ONE OF WIKILEAKS'S ESSENTIAL FEATURES, as Julian Assange has emphatically stressed, is the practice of anonymity. Assange has made this practice the central point of his doctrine and vision of the world. The vocation of WikiLeaks, its raison d'être, is the ambition to construct a site that will assure the impossibility of tracing the individuals who contribute to it. The entire architecture of the organization is meant to guarantee the possibility of acting without a face and with a mask instead. WikiLeaks operates in such a way that those who belong to it cannot know the identity of the "whistle-blowers" who send documents to them; more precisely, they have arranged for their own technical inability to identify these people. This intention amounts to breaking with the classic ethics of journalism, which prescribes that journalists should know their informants. As a general rule, the profession forbids using information that comes from anonymous sources.

WikiLeaks does not know, for instance, whether it was really Chelsea Manning who leaked the diplomatic cables and the video "Collateral Murder." The question does not arise in the world of

WikiLeaks, nor should it. WikiLeaks, Assange says, "is a system that cannot be censored, which enables massive leaks of documents without the risk of being traced."[1] In short, the site is defined as a protected space, hidden and encrypted, which is supposed to foil identification of any and every kind.

The culture of anonymity—the idea of a politics and, more generally, a practice of relating to others without the possibility of the agent being identified—occupies the center of this space of struggle. In particular, it stands at the heart of groups such as Anonymous. One might even say that this protean, unstructured movement is not organized to follow a specific, political line so much as it is a collective shaped by new ways of taking action anonymously. No one knows where the protest comes from, nor can anyone say who belongs to a group that assembles virtually at any given moment to engage with a given cause. This force is unidentifiable. As such, it cannot operate with "established" claims, official "spokespeople," appointed "representatives," and so on.

Frédéric Bardeau and Nicolas Danet have observed that anonymity constitutes a central element of cyberculture—as the use of avatars, in particular, shows. Likewise, they stress that members of Anonymous

> take a sly pleasure in losing observers by sowing confusion, as in a text spread on one of their main channels of communication, "anonews.org": "No one speaks for Anonymous. Nothing is official. No videos. No operations. Not even this press release, even though it was created by an Anonymous number of Anonymous at an Anonymous time in an Anonymous place and uploaded Anonymously, it does not speak for Anonymous."[2]

Choice

This practice of anonymity and of erasing traces should not be viewed as part of an underground tradition of secrecy, which has, after all, been reasonably well chronicled. The point is not simply to escape penalties and consequences.

One might say that Chelsea Manning acted in a concealed manner in order to avoid punishment—to escape repressive measures, and nothing more. By the same token, it might seem that Anonymous wipes away the traces of its activities—which often border on illegality—so as to continue to act without interference. Yet adopting such a view leads to a depoliticization of the practice of anonymity and prevents us from grasping its specificity and its effects. There are frameworks for conducting and understanding political action that determine whether we deem a given activity political or not, whether or not we see it as taking place in a democratic register, and so on. Declaring anonymity to be simply a tactic for pursuing illegal activities while escaping punishment means excluding it from the field of politics. It means marking anonymity as a negative practice endured by those who wield it because it would be too risky for them to do otherwise—that is, not hide. At the same time, such a classification registers the destabilization that our ways of thinking are undergoing; it expresses our implicit expectations with regard to politics. To link anonymity to dissimulation is to remain within the confines of a certain conception of democratic mobilization, formulate outcomes in advance, and give up on understanding other political bearings in anything but negative terms. In other words, it amounts to explaining them only as a deficiency—the result of a constraint or obstacle.

What is at stake in the wake of WikiLeaks or Anonymous, and in the context of what is happening with Chelsea Manning, is a positive conception of anonymity. The point is to *affirm and lay claim to this mode of existence*. WikiLeaks has the avowed objective of promoting the *multiplication of political subjects acting in anonymous fashion*, and it seeks to *give individuals the technical means to do so*. In this manner, the organization explicitly intends to provoke radical action and transform democratic structures and the political sphere. Likewise, for Anonymous, anonymity should not hold for political actions alone; rather, it is the goal for all activities on the Internet, even those of the most everyday or innocuous variety.[3]

What happens when the political subject undertakes action and mobilizes anonymously? What changes does this effect? Needless to say, it would be easy—and there are many, no doubt, who yield to this temptation without further thought—to come up with an un- flattering picture of anonymous actions, one involving "cowardice," denunciation, a lack of courage, and so forth. That said, isn't it pos- sible to chart a different course and call such notions into question? What does branding a certain number of actions in this way teach us about the implicit expectations that we hold for politics and for sub- jects in struggle? In other words: instead of discussing anonymity as a "negative" practice, one may define it as an instrument that enables us to reflect on the framework of our thought and actions. Anonym- ity engages a type of practice and a type of subjectification that cast our unconscious in a critical light; it provides the means to question conventional modalities of political subjectification and expose the effects of power that bear on us through these same channels without our awareness.

Public Space and Democratic Space

In liberal democracies, the question of politics is coextensive with the question of public space. More precisely, it emerges, in essence, in conjunction with the problem of public appearance and visibil- ity: achieving political subjectivity, being a citizen, means engaging and exposing oneself publicly; it means entering public space and bringing a demand, a protest, or a concern *to light*. In saying this, I do not wish to take up Habermas's view of democratic space as a site of discussion and deliberation—what he calls "deliberative democracy"—where the regulated disagreement between individuals finally culminates in the formation of common opinion.[4] The public sphere is a space of struggle, confrontation, and opposition, and the relations that unfold here should be seen as relations of force, not relations of communication. That said, however one pictures democratic space—whether one describes it in terms of opposition or in terms of discussion—the fact remains that it amounts to a stage on which subjects appear and where groups assume positions in relation to each other.

The connection we forge between political activity and the subject's apparition on the so-called public stage is evident in our modes of perception—for instance, the forms of classification we use to define the nature of actions representing an adversarial relationship with the law. Political engagement is often understood as, essentially, the flipside of criminal conduct. But in either case, a conflict with the law is what underlies action. While the criminal seeks to evade the law with which he or she is at odds by means of concealment, the political subject affirms his or her position in the public sphere, voices demands, and works openly to transform the legal order with which he or she stands in conflict. To be sure, many possibilities exist for demonstrating one's disagreement with the legal system. Yet all the same, entering the political realm is seen as necessitating the subject's entry onto the public stage.

Thus, for example, Eric Hobsbawm has asked about the criteria for distinguishing between what he calls "social banditry," that is, illegality that has been integrated into peasant communities and conveys political claims, from "criminal banditry," which refers to ordinary activities outside the law (holdups, looting, and so on). It is striking that, in order to make this distinction, Hobsbawm enlists a problematic of the public sphere, visibility, and daylight. Criminals hide their activities; working at night and under cover of darkness, they live in hiding, behind the scenes. In contrast, sociopolitical bandits do not hide; they go about their activities in full daylight, pursuing their aims openly, publicly, and in plain view.[5] A bandit is social and his actions are political if the banditry is conducted unmasked and out in the open.

Our unconscious, as fashioned by the structures operative in liberal democracies and in political philosophy, links the political and the public. First and foremost, the political sphere is a realm where the subject comes into contact with others and must answer for what he or she says and does. In assuming a position vis-à-vis others, the subject commits his or her name, signature, or voice: signing a petition, showing his or her face, exhibiting his or her social position and related interests, protesting, and so forth.

Hannah Arendt's works, especially *The Human Condition*, exemplify the consubstantiality of politics, public space, and subjectivity—a relationship that lies at the foundation of how we understand the democratic sphere. In effect, Arendt describes public space as the realm where everything may be seen and heard by everyone else.[6] As such, political activity is what unfolds within the sphere where subjects appear and interact openly, under observation; it occurs in the context not only of addressing others, but also of *awaiting* others' *reactions* to what one says and does: "The *polis*, properly speaking, is not the city-state in its physical location; it is the organization of the people as it arises out of acting and speaking together, and its true space lies between people living together for this purpose, no matter where they happen to be." From this perspective, politics is situated in the realm of what appears, or comes into view. The polis, Arendt continues, "is the space of appearance in the widest sense of the word, namely, the space where I appear to others as others appear to me, where men exist not merely like other living or inanimate things but make their appearance explicitly."[7]

This idea that politics is linked, in substance, to public space and, above all, to the gestures of engagement performed here—that is, to a collective scene inhabited by other subjects—orients a significant

portion of contemporary theory and the way it formulates its questions. Accordingly, the matter of politics tends to be approached via
a problematic of appearance, coming-into-view, and visibility (hence
the focus on mass gatherings in public places). How is it that a movement emerges? What are the modalities of its appearance? Who is
watching or listening? What effects, whether lasting or not, do appearance and disappearance produce?

Albert O. Hirschman, for instance, views appearance on the
public stage in terms of the voice—and therefore hearing. In contrast
to apathy and defection, which constitute silent modes of reaction to
dissatisfaction, political activity involves finding the means to make
one's voice heard publicly, issuing demands openly, and expressing
disagreement. Political subjects assert themselves in the public sphere
when dissension enters the expressive register.[8]

Judith Butler, in turn, has recently advanced the body, rather than
the voice, as the medium of engagement—that is, using the context
not of hearing but of vision. For her, the political scene is where bodies assemble and occupy a space. In becoming allied, bodies make
themselves visible; in the process, a "body politic" comes to light.
Politics is inscribed in a problematic of appearance, the engaged presence of bodies on the street, the demonstration of a "we" that, in
occupying the public stage—"places" or "sites"—makes itself visible
and asserts its status as the populace.[9]

Whether they are formulated in terms of vocal enunciation or of
bodily presence, analyses of political activity continue to be domi-
nated by the question of the public sphere and the relationship to
others: politics is thought to be a matter of occupying either a media
space or physical space. It is this engagement of the self, of one's
name, one's voice, one's body—this "publication" of the self as a subject engaged in the struggle, that serves to define political action. As
such, the citizen expressing him- or herself—placing demands, demonstrating, even fighting—is implicitly opposed to the individual

who takes flight or says nothing, who silently accepts the status quo, who breaks the law in secret, and so on.

Being Anonymous

But what if, in the context of Anonymous or an organization like WikiLeaks, we were witnessing the emergence of a practice that puts this entire apparatus into crisis—one that not only destabilizes the ties that have traditionally held among politics, subjects, and the public sphere but, at the same time, enables us to interrogate its functioning, limits, and unreflected moments? The irruption of subjects seeking to act anonymously gives rise to political practices that differ from those that have held until now. It involves laying claim to being otherwise—a movement that unsettles the way the democratic regime operates. We must take this into account and draw our conclusions.

The practice of anonymity enables one to act politically without constituting oneself as an identifiable subject. Anonymous subjects are not subjects who appear. On the contrary, they dissolve as public subjects and organize their own invisibility. When they speak out, block a site, hack, or "demonstrate"—if the word still has any meaning in this context (and indeed, the very vocabulary of politics will need to be reinvented here)—they act, make declarations, and circulate statements without anyone being able to determine where such criticism comes from or who is offering it. The speaking subject does not publicly answer for his or her actions or speech. The "author" of the discourse or action fades away. No place can be assigned to him or her. She or he remains hidden, invisible, and, in consequence, does not come into contact with other subjects. Nothing is visible, or public, except for the acts of mobilization themselves and their effects.

Thus, it is possible for action to be political even when conducted individually, anonymously, and in secret. Chelsea Manning has shown as much. To be sure, action may still be performed collectively—for instance, when Anonymous attacks a site. Even in the latter case, however, we are witnessing a redefinition of the very idea of group mobilization. The protest remains collective, but no group has assembled. Action is carried out individually, by people who are each acting on their own account—unnoticed in an office or home. The "group" amounts to a juxtaposed array of particular actions conducted separately. It does not culminate in any kind of "fusion"; instead, it emerges in the course of struggle, in the moment of combat, and it vanishes again just as soon as the work is done. What is being invented here is political action deployed without reference to the constitution of a "we."

Anonymity, then, enables the field of politics and democracy to be disconnected from the public sphere. Subjects protest and mobilize, but without coming into view—that is, without putting themselves into play as subjects, without stepping before others in the public space as political agents, and without entering a stage shot through with relationships, interpellations, conflicts, and so on. They act by effecting a detachment between their deeds and their persons. In other words, the possibility of acting politically without acting publicly shows—counter to the postulates of conventional political theory—that there is no reason to link politics and publicness. Accordingly, we must question this traditional equation, the reasons why we make it so readily, and what it tells us about our unreflected assumptions.

Anonymity makes it possible to conceive of the subject's relationship to action in a different way. If we appreciate the novelty of what the form of anonymity produces, we have the means to reflect on the limits of the regime that links democratic politics to notions of speaking up, assembly, and appearing or demonstrating in plain sight. In other words, we can question, in critical fashion, the contemporary arrangement (*dispositif*) of politics. What new, virtual political scene has the practice of anonymity brought about? How does it differ from the familiar scene, in which we have grown up and still express ourselves? The quasi-systematic use, in philosophy and the social sciences, of certain concepts to conceive of the political (e.g., "expression," "voice," "collective mobilization," "public sphere," and so on) has a reassuring effect and reinforces a particular representation of democratic space that, in fact, is neither neutral nor self-evident—and contributes to the workings of power and censorship.

Democratizing Access to the Space of Contestation

The economist and legal scholar Balázs Bodó has analyzed the political consequences of the practice of anonymity in "You Have No Sovereignty Where We Gather,"[10] one of the few articles devoted to these questions. Although the piece concerns mobilization on the Internet, larger lessons may be drawn from the discussion. Examining anonymity in the form that WikiLeaks effects, Bodó shows how Julian Assange has lent a new meaning and radicality to the potentials of technology.

Until WikiLeaks, Bodó contends, anonymity was a practice pursued by "outsiders": it enabled individuals scattered across the social spectrum who were unhappy with the way an institution, company, or state operated to manifest their opposition by organizing computerized attacks—notably, "denial-of-service" attacks, which aim to overload a site so that it becomes unavailable for a time.

This mode of protest constitutes a transposition into virtual space of classic forms of collective action: striking, blocking access, sit-ins, and so forth. The point is to obstruct an Internet site just as one obstructs a physical location such as a railway station or public square. Even though the specific features of anonymity and dispersion are already at work in such practices, this form of mobilization still represents a continuation of traditional means of collective action. Moreover, one of today's paramount legal challenges is to give activists who perform this kind of operation the same legal protections that hold for demonstrators out on the street—today, this mode of intervention in virtual space remains criminal, and members of Anonymous have been prosecuted and sentenced to years of prison.

WikiLeaks's historical significance is to have added something new, another use of anonymity that has proven more radical and inventive. In effect, Assange's organization has given itself the task of using the potential of technology to create new ways of rebelling; as such, it promotes the emergence of new political subjects. WikiLeaks has forged a connection between anonymity and the issue of leaks and disclosures by guaranteeing that sources cannot be traced. By design, it is impossible to know the "identity" of individuals who use the service to make information available. Accordingly, Bodó observes, WikiLeaks's goal amounts to introducing new actors to politics: not "outsiders," but "insiders." The point is to enable individuals who belong to an institution—its members—to take political action against this same institution. The function of anonymity is to give insiders the means to transmit institutional information outward, *toward* the public. Moreover, in a more general sense, whistle-blowing represents the emergence of insiders, who are often conformists, as a new kind of protester.

If it is true that the practice of anonymity represents a form of protection, a framework enabling insiders—that is, individuals whose access to this realm was previously de facto blocked—to express themselves in the public sphere, the question follows, as a matter of course, of the extent to which the idea of democracy as it stands serves to produce effects of censorship. Why is it that certain subjects want to—or have to—act anonymously? What are the reasons that a desire for anonymity even exists? In other words: why would appearing in the public eye represent a problem for them? If a demand for anonymity—the will to afford the possibility of acting in this manner—exists, isn't that in order to circumvent the prohibitive or restrictive mechanisms built into the way contemporary politics works?

It would seem that positing a necessary relationship between politics and the public sphere—and therefore demanding that the mobilized subject appear before others—grants importance to political activity by declaring it an essential and prestigious site of human action and fulfillment. In reality, however, this arrangement imposes a limit on conflict and protest. "Engagement" is an apt expression for the unthought dimension at work in our conception of political activity. The implicit assumption is that politics must cost the engaged individual something. We generally tend to accept the view that any political practice worthy of the name should be tied to the subject taking a risk; conversely, we tend to think that if no risk is taken, the activity is less conscious, less dignified—and perhaps less radical, less honest, or even cowardly. Tying politics to the question of the public sphere, positing a connection between democratic practice and the constitution of a realm where a relationship to others is forged, means affirming a kind of pathos of politics. Following this logic, protest demands that one endanger oneself physically, reveal one's identity, and so on. The subject is supposed to commit his or her name or body, be viewed by all, and prove recognizable. Here, we see at work a conception of politics that implicitly involves an idea of dramatic, intensive, and compelling stagecraft.

This scenography, this quasi-sacrificial conception of politics, is what the practice of anonymity calls into question. The anonymous activist incarnates a desire to free him- or herself from such political pathos (which, as Joan W. Scott has shown in the context of women's history, can reinforce fantasmatic identification with figures or scenes of the past[11]). Anonymous subjects give themselves the means to act, but without assuming those modes of action that consecrate the political scenery ratified by any number of theorists who thereby preserve a myth they never examine critically.

Anonymity serves to lower the objective and psychic costs of politics. To be sure, this does not mean that one cannot be identified and punished—indeed, ferocious state repression currently targets the actions undertaken by Anonymous. Here, however, my interest is in the aspirations that account for recourse to anonymity and the relation they entertain with the invention of new political subjectivity and a new political scene. (Whereby, as we will see, efforts to quash such activity may be explained as reactions to the destabilization produced by the irruption of new modes of action.)

Intervening without making an appearance means trying to protect oneself from the risks that engagement entails—the risks, for instance, of reprimand, demotion, or firing. Politics in the traditional configuration demands a high price from those who act. In consequence, a significant question arises: why should it be that politics costs (me) anything? Why should I commit myself to a cause—or, more precisely, why should a cause *commit me*? I bear no responsibility for the dysfunctions that I reveal. Fundamentally, setting up a scene where protest costs, or is supposed to cost, the subject—or going after those whose investment in a cause counts as "cowardly" (or as not truly committed)—amounts to positing that loyalty or conformism represents a normal stance and is unproblematic; conversely, it means that dissent is a *choice* for which I am to be made *responsible*. For instance: why should Chelsea Manning, after observing mounting instances of illegality within the army, have appeared in public and risked her career, retaliation, and so on? She held no responsibility for the dysfunctions. Constructing an arrangement in which political action necessarily assumes a form that commits and implicates the individuals who perform it amounts to making them take an objective or subjective risk for the sake of something for which they hold no responsibility.

The practice of anonymity reveals that the idea of democracy we know and observe produces censoring effects: it means that fewer subjects speak, and it blocks some subjects from acting at all. Tying politics to publicness and constructing the political scene as a stage for dramatic appearances, confrontation, or collective mobilization sets up an order that, for a whole array of individuals, restricts the possibility of speaking up, achieving self-expression, or acting. It is too risky, too costly, to do so. In contrast, the apparatus of anonymity should enable the redistribution of the right to speak by lessening the cost of politics—or, more precisely, by undoing the very idea that politics should cost those who act anything at all. As such, movements that lay claim to anonymity advance something like a demand to radicalize democratic principles by changing modes of access to politics and transforming the political scene—that is, by eliminating certain nondemocratic barriers entailed by the conventional understanding of democracy. Chelsea Manning could act only because there was anonymity. Anonymity is what made her existence possible in the first place—a technique for creating "Chelsea Manning," for creating protesting political subjects.

Destabilizing Institutions

If anonymity democratizes the conditions of access to democracy and thereby puts the traditional political scene into crisis, this is not only because it lifts certain censoring effects produced by the traditional configuration of politics. In addition, I believe, it occurs because the possibility for acting anonymously introduces a break in the interplay of politics and identity: anonymity enables individuals who would not describe themselves as "politicized" to perform acts of protest, too.

Inasmuch as politics takes place via one's appearance in the public sphere, it fosters the construction of a certain social identity—a certain way of being viewed by others and allying oneself with others. It is no accident that, in the main, contemporary political activity involves mobilized groups that define themselves as such (unions, nonprofit organizations, and the like). When the subject engages in political action, it means assuming a public role: being perceived—and *constituted*—as such by others, which in turn leads to the crystallization and solidification of identity through the interplay of others' perspective and one's own self-perception. The "public" nature of the political sphere explains what one might deem the institutionalized nature of protest, that is, the existence of agents specialized in democratic struggle who simultaneously bring it to life and monopolize it.

Anonymity, in contrast, permits a kind of social disembedding of active engagement: political activity no longer imposes identification; it ceases to yield a stable identity that one must assume vis-à-vis others—for instance, in a hierarchy or among colleagues, friends, or family. Being an activist or a militant no longer represents a visible quality: political action becomes provisional; it no longer amounts to an abiding commitment. Anonymity offers isolated individuals, who have no particular partisan orientation or established political loyalty, the means to decide, at any given moment, whether to protest against the institution to which they belong by leaking information. It enables those who would not define themselves in oppositional, radical, or militant terms—or who do not wish to define themselves in this way—to enter the sphere of political protest.

This arrangement changes the nature and form of protest. Inasmuch as anyone is able to engage in protest on his or her own, invisibly, it represents a transitory and fragmentary practice: a subject takes action at a particular point and, at the same time, remains completely aligned with the institution. Anonymity permits the subject not to be implicated in what she or he does (or, at any rate, not entirely). Thanks to anonymity, the source of leaks (among other things) cannot be identified. Henceforth, protest can arise anywhere, at any time, and without anyone being able to know where it comes from or to foresee it. *Everyone* is able to participate at one point or another. There are no longer any sites of mobilization—nor, more specifically, organizations (such as unions) that are clearly identified as the instances from which protest issues.

In essence, the emergence of new political figures such as Anonymous or individuals who, like Chelsea Manning, secretly upload information via WikiLeaks, signifies a process of redistribution and scattering of the sites of protest. This phenomenon is likely to produce extremely powerful destabilizing effects on the workings of power in contemporary societies, the relationship between individuals and institutions, and the processes of demonstrating allegiance.

Scattering

Didier Eribon has shown that if we wish to grasp instances of subversion, the sites where something subversive occurs, we must look for phenomena that shift the borders between the inside and the outside, the center and the margin, the "conventional" and the "dissenting."[12] What is particular to the practice of anonymity is that it is capable of constituting every member of an institution as someone who can *potentially* be—whether at one and the same time, or in turn—both "in" and "out," both in conformity and politicized, in a position of both adherence and protest.[13] Such a situation makes institutions more fragile than does the ritual confrontation that occurs between antagonists that are identified, in keeping with codified procedures. If the emergence of anonymity favors the possibility of protest coming from anywhere, at any time, and on the part of anyone, it is clear how it may promote the expansion of forms of protest, occasion a deinstitutionalization of politics, and perhaps, in so doing, free up and foster forces of dissent.

(It is, moreover, striking that, in the last few years, numerous governments, companies, and administrations have adopted regulations that promise to protect "whistle-blowers" on the condition that they disclose improprieties they have observed through channels internal to the organization in question—that is, that they direct concerns to an identified office or service. These arrangements have the purpose of checking, and blocking, the amount of information disclosed to organizations such as WikiLeaks. Thus, it is clear that there is now a whole array of efforts to reestablish traditional channels of protest and of the voicing of criticism.)

Duplicity

It is also possible to describe the destabilizing force of anonymity in another way: by trading the institutional viewpoint for the subject's perspective. The fact that subjects can perform anonymous political actions directed against an organization while belonging to that same organization represents a crisis for the psychic regime on which institutions are based and through which they exercise their hold.

Reflecting on how the social and political order functions and reproduces itself has made it clear how important the interplay of techniques is for engendering the identification of subjects with the institutions to which they belong. What Michel Foucault calls "subjugation" refers to mechanisms whose purpose is to cause individuals to tie the relationship they have with themselves—the ways they see themselves—to how institutions view them.[14] We are fashioned in such a way that we tend to adhere subjectively to the insitutions to which we objectively belong, inasmuch as we accept a certain number of narratives, images of self and others, values, and so on. All institutions function thanks to operations of "identification."

But couldn't the practice of anonymity represent a force capable of jamming this mechanism of incorporation? Having an avatar, a pseudonym—being able to intervene in a concealed fashion—makes it possible to cultivate a kind of recalcitrance toward the institutions to which one belongs. The mere existence of the possibility for contesting the institution of which one forms a part enables practices of contradictory allegiance that are potentially in conflict with each other. Fundamentally, organizations like WikiLeaks mean to produce a new kind of subjectification: *split* subjectification. They provide individuals the means to be, at one and the same time, within an institution and anonymously engaged in activities that promote values that are contrary to, or that protest, this same institution. Anonymity enables the subject to belong to an institution while entertaining a form of exteriority with regard to it. It makes it possible to cultivate forms of *duplicity*.

From here on, anonymity might indeed function as an interface that offers subjects the possibility of protecting themselves, of maintaining a kind of psychic security with regard to the institution, of avoiding identifying with it—of remaining engaged in other worlds and other practices even while still belonging to the institution. Far from resembling cowardice, anonymous action would be the starting point for learning resistance and lucidity. In providing the means to belong, simultaneously, to several mental universes, it enables the possibility of playing them out against each other and, in this way, to put to work a process of dis-identification and de-simplification of oneself vis-à-vis institutions: to promote practices that are freer and more selective—more and more emancipated from the psychic hold of external and arbitrary constraints. Thus, we could consider "anonymity" the term for a technique of desubjugation.

Affirming Conflictuality

I wish to conclude this investigation of the stakes of inventing anonymous political subjectivity and of what laying claim to anonymity might portend by reflecting on the very form of democratic activity and social confliction. Anonymity does not merely entail the multiplication of subjects engaged in struggle and the redistribution of the sites of protest. It can, in equal measure, redefine the contours of the democratic sphere, that is, the way we conceive it and the relations we are able to establish within it. The will to struggle politically and anonymously harbors the will to bring to life a new conception of politics and protest.

Relatively little attention is paid to the fact that conceiving the political dimension in terms of public appearance implicitly presumes that all acts of protest must necessarily be based on a sphere of interaction with those one is forced to fight against. In fact, declaring politics to be an arena where the subject is constituted in plain view, where she or he appears and intervenes, means locating politics in the order of relationality. Constituting oneself as a political subject, whether individually or collectively, is necessarily supposed to entail establishing a relationship with others. Indeed, according to Arendt, it is the establishment of this relation—that is, transforming something private into something public, with all the risk it entails—that defines the point of origin of politics.[15]

To be sure, the relation to others can assume many different forms. It may involve discussion and communication or, alternatively, conflict and confrontation. But either way, however one pictures the scene—whether as dialogue or struggle—linking politics to one's appearance in the public sphere means tying politics to one's appearance before others; that is, it means positing a kind of submission to others as the very condition for political action. Displaying one's body out on the street or opening one's mouth to speak represent acts through which one addresses the other de facto: I call on him or her, provoke his or her reaction, I expect something of him or her, and so on. In entering the political realm, the subject enters an intersubjective sphere, as well. In a word, the subject establishes a point of contact, a connection.

Thus, writing on conflict, Georg Simmel stressed that, contrary to appearances and the superficial interpretations proposed by reactionary authors, political struggles do not represent an instance of rupture between the parties facing off. They do not constitute a moment of "untying" that signifies what conservatives call a "crisis" of the "social" bond. Instead, they stand for a moment of integration, because, in fact, subjects in struggle, when they take a position in the space of protest, are addressing the adversary; they demonstrate that a response is expected: they show that they acknowledge their opponents, view them as interlocutors, are ready to negotiate with them, and so on.[16]

Although it is not critical, Simmel's analysis enables us to understand the paradoxes of traditional, political action and its implicit presuppositions. When a subject exposes a conflict publicly, when she or he assumes a position openly in conflict with a group or institution, she or he in fact occupies the register of address: a scene of dialogue emerges. From the very moment a conflict comes into view, everything that happens happens as if the conflict had to be covered up—or, more precisely, as if the only condition for accepting the conflict were for the rivals to have stripped the antagonisms that it aimed to expose of their intensity and relegated them to the background so that the rivals might acknowledge each other as mutual interlocutors within a shared world.

One of the things that makes anonymity powerful—that explains the desire to which this mode of subjectification gives rise—lies in its capacity to liberate us from the demand of entertaining a relationship with those with whom we stand in conflict. Anonymous action enables the formation of conflict free from reciprocity of any kind. Acting anonymously means being able not to appear to others and not to engage in interaction with the party one is forced to fight. It is not a matter of refusing relationality in general, but of acting in such a way that there is no need to establish an undesired relationship—and, to be sure, of not accepting that politics requires one to yield to this kind of constraint. This practice makes it possible to radicalize and intensify conflicts while refusing to pretend that no conflict exists.

Anonymity means being freed of the ethical scene. Accordingly, one can readily imagine why groups and individuals who practice it seek to cast off the traditional framework of politics in order to find a new one. On this new stage, politics would not operate by way of negotiation or communication. Instead, it would be an *affirmative* politics: voicing one's claims, acting, then vanishing. Masks and encryption enable intervention without establishing a relationship, without acknowledging one's enemies or giving them the possibility to respond. Anonymous, for instance, is a collective that mobilizes at a given moment for a specific cause; the group has no definition, contours, unity, or identity. It dissolves as soon as the action is terminated. It is immanent to the struggle.

One strand of contemporary theory, "recognition theory," which is in the Hegelian tradition, aims to think politics as a component of ethics. The objective is to develop the idea that political relations are always structured, in terms of content and goal alike, by ethical concerns. This analytical framework means reading every conflict by starting with a nonpolitical language—that is, interpreting every struggle as if, behind the demands explicitly voiced by actors (whether they are material in nature or not), there were always an ethical search for recognition, for the construction of a sphere of communication. In a word, politics is supposed to be the site where the desire for reciprocity finds expression.[17]

Subjects who act anonymously exhibit, in practical terms, the will to put another idea of politics into operation. Their actions disrupt the Hegelian scheme of recognition, which describes neither an anthropological fact nor a structure of desire but merely ratifies an instituted order of operations in the political field and the subjectivities fashioned there (as if politics and subjectivity were all there was). Anonymous subjects endeavor to escape this contamination of politics by ethics and to enable struggles that are freed from any obsessive concern with the gaze of others. By disconnecting the question of politics from the question of the public sphere, anonymity gives rise to a scene on which what one might call nonrelational politics occurs: politics that is affirmative and radically emancipated from all ethical considerations—in other words, perhaps, pure politics.

CHAPTER 5

FLIGHT AND THE POLITICS OF BELONGING

NEEDLESS TO SAY, what has just been said about the logic of anonymity does not apply to Julian Assange or Edward Snowden. In effect, the editor-in-chief of WikiLeaks has always been public about the actions his organization undertakes and the doctrine he advocates. Likewise, and in a more interesting way, Snowden did not act in the same manner as Chelsea Manning, nor did he combine his repeated gesture of disclosing information with a desire for anonymity. On the contrary, he *wanted* to take the stage as the source of leaks. He has consistently sought to reveal his identity and account for his reasons, motivations, and intentions. Thus, in *No Place to Hide*, Glenn Greenwald tells how, when he met Snowden with film director Laura Poitras and talked about the information he had to share, his interlocutor consistently affirmed that he wanted to be known as the source so he could explain why he had acted as he did:

> He insisted on identifying himself as the source of the documents, and on doing so publicly in the first article we published. "Anyone who does something this significant has the obligation

to explain to the public why he did it and what he hopes to
achieve," he said. He also did not want to heighten the climate
of fear the US government had fostered by hiding.[1]

Accordingly, in the video interview that appeared on the *Guardian*
website on 9 June 2013, Snowden explains his course of action to
Greenwald and tells the world that he was the one who provided
the information that the *Guardian* and the *Washington Post* had published a few days prior.

Inasmuch as Assange and Snowden have taken the stage in the
public eye, claimed responsibility for their actions, and appeared in
the media, one cannot deny that they occupy positions in the traditional and familiar forms of politics. But all the same, alongside
this image that conforms to established practice, something is happening that breaks with the established political order. Assange and
Snowden also incarnate a mode of subjectification that defies the law
and the state, even though the modality at work differs from that of
anonymity.

Assange and Snowden appear in the public sphere, to be sure.
That said, they do so in a singular fashion, because they have tied
their course of action to a practice of flight, of seeking refuge and
asylum. The political gestures they perform have been systematically
linked to migratory activity. Thus, when Snowden wanted to make
himself known, he made a video—but he did so from abroad. He
met with Greenwald in Hong Kong: only from there did he claim
responsibility for his actions. Moreover, it was only after fleeing the
United States and seeking refuge in another country that he even
revealed his identity. In other words, a key feature of what Snowden
did involved escaping from the United States and assuring that he
could never be extradited. Likewise, Assange has constantly changed
countries. He has always linked his desire to pursue his activism to
questioning his place of residence, in order to find a political and

legal system likely to offer the guarantees and protections he needs. This is why he has lived in Australia, Germany, and England— where, in London, he found refuge at the embassy of Ecuador on 19 June 2012.

This readiness to escape and this practice of seeking asylum strike me as extremely significant, for they entail a number of consequences for our thinking and for the ways we conceive of the ethics of belonging, engagement, and territoriality. At first glance, these matters might seem to be anecdotal or even to represent an unproblematically transparent gesture with a self-evident meaning: that Assange and Snowden are simply seeking to assure that they go unpunished and avoid penal sanctions. Such considerations are hardly wrong. At the same time, however, it would be mistaken to content ourselves with these all-too-obvious interpretations.

The practice of seeking asylum—its intimate connection to political action, expatriation, and the call for protection—raises important problems. There is something at play here that amounts to a questioning of the support we often spontaneously accord national systems. In a very concrete way, Snowden and Assange have enacted a mode of revolt that allows us to think differently about the category of the political, its limits, and the relationship we entertain with the state. They give us the means to view the political domain as harboring problems that are otherwise excluded—and to radicalize the question of democracy by taking into account the problems of inclusion, nationality, and citizenship.

The Nonpolitical Foundations of Political Theory

In order to begin my reflections, I must start with a seeming paradox of political philosophy. It is striking to observe the extent to which theory tends to consign the question of communities, shared belongings, and borders to a space outside of politics. Thinking about democracy, or conceptions of the state, is all too often restricted to studying forms of government; this, in turn, is supposed to provide a scene of debate and evaluation for types of regime, modalities of collective decision making, laws and their improvement, individual rights, the limits of sovereignty, work toward common interest, and so on.

To be sure, analyzing the nature of the laws to which we are subject is essential. That said, however, shouldn't political philosophy also examine, and just as thoroughly, the simple fact that we are subject to them in the first place—and by what right this has occurred? Shouldn't it place at the center of investigation the question of belonging to such-and-such a political entity, the fact that we belong to it along with others, and the foundations underpinning such an order?

Sometimes, writings on democracy seem to want to extend the democratic sphere to everything . . . except that which concerns the borders between political groups and the right of individuals to get rid of them. This line of questioning is not open to debate—it has been excluded from the field of politics. Borders and issues of belonging are established as matters of fact, as simply given. In essence, the frame of thinking set forward by Rousseau prevails: human beings are compelled to gather together and people therefore hold a common stake in the grouping imposed on them; *The Social Contract* is a meditation on ways to transform the cluster of human beings defined in this way, where everyone must live, into a populace possessing a legitimate constitution.

The Contract

Depoliticizing the question of belonging, then, would appear to underlie political philosophy and to provide the field with its objects of inquiry. This also holds for contractualism, in particular, including the version elaborated by John Rawls. Rawls formulates the matter explicitly and renews the gesture of depoliticization that had already been made by Rousseau and Kant. That said, it is not entirely clear why he does so—after all, it stands to undermine his project and the idea of democracy on which he means to base his enterprise as a whole.

Contractual philosophers exclude the question of *who it is we make the contract with*. Society counts as closed; living with one another, we must find a system that is just and suitable for all. In other words, the problems Rawls addresses are underpinned by a national unconscious, or implicit nationalism, which leads him to view the borders of the communities in which we live and the nature of the communities to which we belong as a nonpolitical issue.[2] Thus, he writes, "we begin with principles of political justice for the basic structure of a closed and self-contained liberal democratic society."[3] As Rawls pictures things, citizens belong to a system that is discrete and separate from other societies. This isolation, this closure, explains the emergence of the question of how the polis is organized—the need for a theory of justice and, ultimately, the way to resolve matters.

All in all, then, one might even ask whether the critical analysis of forms of government and juridical systems that Rawls's theory of justice is supposed to afford simply follows from his failure to problematize modes of belonging. Would the questions take the same form if Rawls did not exclude the issue of the borders that define communities? The problem of administering political space, the issue of enabling the coexistence of a plurality of groups (religious, ethnic, and so on) adhering to contradictory and even antagonistic values, and the question of the limits on one group's interference in the affairs of another are meaningful only because of the presupposition that these groups should live together, or already do so, and should be subject to the same legislation. In other words, the field of investigation is already defined in terms that exclude the possibility that these groups do not constitute one and the same legal entity and have chosen to form communities that are in part distinct.

Cohabitation

Judith Butler also excludes from the field of politics the question of the borders that define who comprises a community. Even though she addresses matters that are as far as possible from the legal reasoning and problems that interest Rawls, she engages in the same depoliticization of belonging. Thus, *Parting Ways* takes issue with contractualism; by placing the category of cohabitation at the center of reflection, Butler seeks to base political theory on foundations other than contracts and the ontology of individual will.

In Butler, cohabitation represents a condition of human existence: the "we" constituting the political community is held to be marked, from its inception, by an irreducible plurality that politics should attempt not to contain or reduce, but to preserve, if not increase. Butler's proposal leads to a critique of the nation-state in the name of federation. However, the consequence of this analysis is to transfer the question of "we"—the matter of knowing who else belongs to "us"—to the register of ontology, or even geography. At any rate, it still entails rejecting questions of how the "we" comes to be situated outside politics. To be sure, Butler opposes contractualism, yet at the same time she, too, voices the idea that the group through which we form a community lies outside the political realm. Indeed, she concludes that we are inscribed within a system from which there is no escaping—one that is "closed," as Rawls would say; in consequence, she declares, we should organize it politically. For Rousseau, such prepolitical circumstances, which are to be administered politically, represent the state of nature. For Rawls, they are a given: a fact posited by theory. For Butler, they constitute an ethical condition.

Butler writes: "The liberal framework according to which each of us enters into a contract knowingly and voluntarily does not take into account that we are already living on the earth with those we never chose."[4] She continues: "This means that unwilled proximity and unchosen cohabitation are preconditions of our political existence, which is the basis of [Arendt's] critique of the nation-state (and its presumption of a homogeneous nature), and implies the obligation to live on the earth and in a polity that establishes modes of equality for a necessarily heterogeneous population."[5] In other words, Butler makes the notion of unchosen cohabitation an instrument for critiquing contractualism: "This way of being bound to one another is precisely *not* a social bond that is entered into through volition and deliberation; it precedes contract, is mired in interdependency, and is often effaced by those forms of social contract that presume and instate an ontology of volitional individuals."[6] At the same time, however—as is also the case for Rawls—those with whom we form a society count as always already given.

If Butler insists on situating the ethical necessity of living alongside those with whom we share the world, without our having had a say in the matter, she clearly does so because of the particular situation analyzed in her extremely important book: the Israeli-Palestinian conflict, the Occupied Territories, the rights of Palestinians, and so on. But in order to do so, Butler enlists classic notions of political philosophy and makes certain, traditional ways of formulating problems her own. For Butler, cohabitation represents a quasi-geographical given and an ethical condition, and it is starting from the demands that this entails that we must construct a legal system capable of protecting human plurality instead of reducing it—or, worse still, denying it altogether.

Depoliticization

This way of understanding and confronting the question of politics is inscribed within a strangely limiting framework: what does it mean to establish a political philosophy on the basis of the nonpolitical? Isn't it problematic to develop a theory of democracy from factors—in particular, belonging and co-belonging—that are nondemocratic and, as such, do not admit choice or deliberation inasmuch as they derive from the ontological order, are simply given, correspond to geographical situations, and so on? Doesn't it warrant criticism when the borders of political communities are consigned to a place outside the field of democracy? Is there any relying on a political theory that bases its edifice on a nonpolitical fact—that is, in reality, on an act of depoliticization?

Needless to say, this problem is not abstract or purely speculative. It has practical consequences for the way we conceive of ourselves, how we view our relationship to others, and our mode of attaining political subjectivity. Not politicizing the question of belonging— relegating the problem of the form of community in which we are situated to a realm outside of politics—forces us to accept a matter that is purely arbitrary and without meaning as intangible, tran- scendent reality. Not problematizing the question of belonging—or, more precisely, failing to give oneself the means to see this question as potentially problematic—means implicating oneself in a position of constraint, resigning oneself to a contingent situation: the fact that we were born in this particular country, and not another, and have this particular nationality. When political philosophy confronts us with the question of organizing the polis, it presumes that what hap- pens where I was born concerns me and that I should face what oc- curs there as a matter of course.

The Power of Sedition

It is impossible to satisfy modes of thinking that involve taking a certain number of realities as given and deducing obligations from them—as if the framework that is supposed to govern our lives were not subject to deliberation and followed logically from phenomena over which we exercise no influence.

The function of politics—and therefore of political theory, as well—is to enable us to retake possession of what is imposed on us and to expand the space of democracy, which is to say the space of choice. Herein lies the grandeur displayed by Snowden and Assange. They represent political subjects in the strong sense of the word, that is, they are politicizing questions that have been depoliticized and, in so doing, mounting an attack on the heart of the juridico-political system. In fleeing, migrating, and explicitly refusing to stand before the justice of "their" country (is it still even their country?), they reject national or political belonging and the manner in which it has been imposed on them. They affirm the right to detach themselves from "their" community (*faire sédition de "leur" communauté*). They radicalize the demand for democracy by publicly proclaiming the right to choose their own community: they reject the depoliticizing construction of belonging handed down by political theory and shift this question into the realm of choice—or, at any rate, of relative choice.

As such, the practice of flight calls into question what one could call the *national structures of revolt and politics*. This expression is not meant to refer to the fact that the objectives and rhythms of dissent are largely organized within a nation, or that few movements unfold on an international scale with international goals. Instead, the point is to bring to light how much established modes of protest and, more generally, the understanding we have of the concept of politics are based on the ratification of our own legal belonging and nationality. As commonly practiced, politics is based on depoliticizing the problem that we are inscribed as subjects of the state.

The vocabulary of political action invokes, almost exclusively, notions of resistance, opposition, and revolution. Classifying an act as political calls for confronting problems collectively, mobilizing in order to transform the state of things or of laws. The great forms of collective action exemplify a spontaneous understanding of this kind: when facing a situation with which we disagree, what do striking, petitions, or demonstrations mean? All these responses amount to viewing our membership in the "community" in which the conflict has arisen as a self-evident matter and not calling it into question. Engagement, confrontation, mobilization, and the discussion of the law or juridico-political regime presuppose acknowledging the nation or nation-state as the space to which one belongs, within which one defines oneself as a subject. Every act of revolt within a group presumes, on the part of the person who performs it, the ratification of his or her belonging to the group: deeming it his or her own or, in other words, reinforcing the idea that the community is self-evident.

In contrast, fleeing means casting off this belonging, refusing it—and thereby calling into question the legal mechanisms of inclusion within a national community, and indeed, in a more general sense, the mechanisms of inclusion in other kinds of groups that are supposed to contain us. It is a mode of subjectification that does not rely on a ratification of its inscription within the national order but demands that inscription be suspended, called into question, in order to grant oneself the right not to face the world with which one disagrees, to practice sedition—or, in an extreme case, to no longer feel concerned. Flight may represent one of the few forms of struggle that problematize the question of belonging without considering it to be self-evident.

Rogues

The singular nature of the practice of flight or sedition appears quite clearly when compared to civil disobedience. Flight and disobedience represent the two extremes of the art of revolt, for they imply opposite modes of subjectification: different ways for the subject to relate to the law, the state, and others.

Writings on civil disobedience—for instance by Jacques Derrida—always tie the grandeur of the practice to the fact that it means making a society confront itself: using its fundamental values, its constitution, in order to critique laws or their current form of organization. The decision to adopt a dissenting attitude is made in the name of loyalty to the essential values of the nation (and this notion of "community spirit" or of "shared values" seems problematic to me). Civil disobedience seeks to perfect the law of the national community. In other words, the subject constitutes him- or herself as a political subject by affirming his or her belonging to the legal community she or he addresses. In a sense, this means presenting oneself as its most faithful member, the one most attached to its values: taking up the fight in their name and in the name of the demands they represent.

But taking flight, seeking refuge, leaving altogether—as Snowden did—means constituting oneself as a political subject in a different way. If one radicalizes this gesture and tries to follow its logic all the way through, it is clear that, for Snowden, the stakes are not to change *his* political community but to change the political community, period. The person who disobeys adheres to his or her nation and means to transform its laws. In contrast, Snowden—and one could show the same of Assange—is committed to a practice of desubjugation that has led him to stop belonging to his nation: at some point, he decided to go, to leave it behind. This was less an act of disobedience than an act of resignation. Snowden's life does not tell of disobedience in order to change the political community, but of changing one's state of belonging: "I'm going somewhere else, leaving this political community, rejecting my nationality." Hence the many asylum requests he has made.

It is clear why it would be inadequate—and even normative and regressive—to call Snowden's gesture a matter of "civil disobedience" (if not simply disobedience), and why, on the contrary, it must be called a *practice* of flight. Disobedience represents a paradox relative to the community where it occurs. Viewing the act one performs as disobedience means inscribing oneself in the system of the law—acknowledging that this law should apply to one, even while deciding not to follow it. In other words, it is impossible to disobey a law without recognizing it as one's own and, in so doing, accepting one's inscription in the community it rules. Max Weber stressed this very point when discussing thieves: they only *seem* to jeopardize the law, because their mode of action actually *confirms* the legal system and the efficacy of the legal order. "A thief," Weber writes, "orients his action to the validity of the criminal in that he acts surreptitiously. The fact that the order is recognized as valid in his society is made evident by the fact that he cannot violate it openly without punishment."[7]

Snowden, on the other hand, has pursued a course that involves freeing himself from the order of the law, abandoning the field where it applies—the realm of *enforcement*—and, in so doing, refusing to define himself in relation to it (or, more precisely, *trying* to free himself from the legal order in which he was born, because no one can ever leave it entirely, one might always be called back, and one can only abandon it by submitting to another one). It is no longer *his* law—that's not his concern. Taking flight, refusing one's inscription in the legal system means adopting the stance of a subject who exercises the right to no longer consider the law as his or her own, with all the obligations it entails.

Thus, claiming that Snowden disobeyed would amount to a grave error with regard to the gesture he performed and its nature and implications. Worse still, it would mean reinscribing him in a legal order that he challenged and repudiated when he said, in effect, "I'm leaving—I belong to another world, I demand asylum." In a word, it would amount to subjugating him again to the legal order from which he resolved to liberate himself.

In taking flight and seeking asylum, Snowden made himself a political subject who exercises the right of sedition. Likewise, Assange has not stopped migrating from one place to another, seeking a territority suited to his values and compatible with his life and political project. These figures are thus the embodiment of legal subjects that retain the right to refuse the law. They reject the system of judgment that has taken repressive measures against them: they refuse to submit and to appear before the law. To designate such a position of foreignness vis-à-vis laws and rights, Derrida has employed the category of *rogue*.[8] Indeed, it may be that Snowden and Assange have called to life an ethics of the rogue to counteract the ethics of citizenship.

In law courts, one of the most common phrases one is likely to hear from a defendant—which sums up the type of subjectification demanded of the legal subject—is, "I take responsibility for my actions. I have faith in my country's judicial system." In contrast, Assange and Snowden have broken with such spontaneous submission to national institutions by declaring: "I don't trust the law of my country, and, what's more, this isn't the law of my country—it's not my country anymore, I've left."

Snowden and Assange politicize a question that is normally depoliticized: to what community do I belong? Why? And by what right? Why should the state decide for me? I believe it is necessary to take a radical stance here, and I would like to propose the idea that we are witnessing, today, the birth of a new political category for individuals who are not defined by their membership in a state, or a nation, or a territory, but rather belong to a community they have chosen for themselves: democracy. When their democratic ideals come into conflict with their membership in a nation, these "citizens of democracy" divorce themselves from their state and find ways to continue their activities—by seeking asylum, for example. What we are witnessing, then, foreshadows a kind of politics that is no longer imagined as an organization of a territory, a city, or as the performative constitution of a "we," as is almost always otherwise the case. Politics now becomes a practice in which new political communities are produced, and imagined, and in which membership or belonging is not situated at the beginning of the process, but at the end. It is not the point of departure but the point of arrival. I propose to designate this process as a "denationalization of the mind." Perhaps we may even find here the possibility of realizing Marx's aspiration and giving birth to what he called the "International."

Belonging

The attitude of sedition calls into question the legal order and our spontaneous submission to it. It takes aim at the heart of the juridico-political order by contesting the initial dispossession we suffer when it imposes its legislation and constitutes us as one of its subjects. Only the radicalism of this interrogation can account for the declarations made by U.S. Secretary of State John Kerry against Snowden. Significantly, Kerry did not use his harshest language to denounce the revelations or to claim that Snowden, in unveiling state secrets, had undermined the war on terror, but instead saved his most savage rhetoric to criticize Snowden's flight—his refusal to stand and face American justice. Snowden, in Kerry's eyes, is a "traitor"—not because he made information public, but because he fled abroad. Other whistle-blowers, Kerry claims, have acted as "patriots": they did not leave, but faced charges in U.S. courts and defended their actions. Snowden, in contrast, is a "coward." What is more, Kerry declares, "If this man is a patriot, he should stay in the United States and make his case. Patriots don't go to Russia, they don't seek asylum in Cuba, they don't seek asylum in Venezuela, they fight their cause here."[9]

That said, one has every right to ask in turn: why does Snowden owe anything to the United States? How is it that he has the least commitment to this state? On what basis can one make the extravagant claim that the American courts represent the justice of "his" country, or that he should accept being judged by them—and, in the process, risking punishment beyond measure? Why should he live in the United States, and not Cuba or Venezuela? Kerry's rhetoric involves acting as if a wholly contingent situation (one's site and date of birth) dictated (moral) obligations for the subject. Here, two attitudes, two *politics*, stand opposed: Kerry is invoking, ratifying, and insisting on forced inclusion, whereas Snowden intends to free himself from the same and to refuse it by fleeing.

Implications

An analysis of social and political violence must address the objective injunctions that serve to produce subjective adherence to arbitrary points of belonging. (Kerry's declarations represent one manifestation of such injunctions in the political order.) A whole array of discursive operations weighs on us, aiming to force us to occupy a position vis-à-vis realities that are *supposed* to concern us and make us accountable for circumstances for which, in fact, we bear no responsibility—and which we may deem utterly foreign to ourselves. One of the primary principles underlying how the world works is to constrain individuals to adhere to places assigned by the arbitrary fact of birth; subjects should come to recognize them as their own inasmuch as injunctions, demands, evaluations, and so forth bind them to these positions and attendant circumstances. Such mechanisms of implication assert themselves as calls to order precisely when the subject seeks to rid him- or herself of assigned positions and grant him- or herself other identities and subjective coordinates.

From this point of view, one might draw an analogy between the situation described and the "class defector." When someone is perceived as a defector, she or he is often faulted for having taken flight individually—that is, for having left behind "his" or "her" social group instead of mobilizing to change the system as a whole. Sartre, for instance, offers such an analysis in "Materialism and Revolution"[10] when discussing social mobility and the securing of membership in the bourgeoisie. In *Exit, Voice, Loyalty*, Albert O. Hirschman refers to the polemics that arose in the Black community concerning people who advanced to privileged positions and joined "white society" instead of contributing to the "'collective stimulation' of blacks as a group."[11]

For the discussion at hand, the question is why the matter of class (or race) comes up so intensely for people who have been born working class (or black). Why should a purely contingent matter entail any particular duties, concerns, or practices?

If black issues or the labor question are political matters, this is so *for everyone and all the time*. As such, the dilemma of individual social mobility and collective struggle against structures of domination represents a *false problem* based on converting contingent facts into significant ones; this means making the subject responsible for situations exterior to him- or herself, or, more exactly, making him or her accountable and answerable to them—that is, situate him- or herself with respect to them.

Such a perspective was widely adopted (though not always in a negative way) apropos of Édouard Louis when he published *The End of Eddy*.[12] Why was Louis asked how he was helping to dismantle the structure of social classes (and at the very moment when he was exposing prevailing conditions, at that)? Casting Louis's book in this problematic light amounted to calling for a return to order, to trying to restore this subject to his original position by demanding that he recognize the place assigned at birth as his own, or, more precisely, as the point of reference for situating and viewing his own life—instead of acknowledging that it has given him the means to emancipate and invent himself freely.

A Democratic Critique of the law

It is not my intention to limit my reflections to the compass of Snowden and Kerry. Kerry made the declarations of a statesman—they represent a conception of the state in keeping with unconscious notions that are widely and deeply rooted in the popular mind. Such statements hold interest inasmuch as they express what one might call the integrative violence of the state and national belonging.

It is surely accurate to describe the law as a rational instance that fosters liberty and protects individuals' capacity to act. That said, valorizing this dimension alone amounts to covering up the restricted nature of the situation that makes this positive gain possible. After all, one's first experience of one's relationship to the state is a matter of imposition, an obligation: one is born in a state, hence one has no choice but to be its subject. There is no element of choice in being subject to the legal order.

First and foremost, the question of the state is a question of obligatory belonging. The violence of the juridico-political order does not reside in the instances of exclusion or dispossession to which it gives rise so much as in the inclusions it decrees. The status of citizen represents an imposition before it becomes a promotion. Without being asked, without having formally or contractually expressed my will, I am de facto inscribed in the state as subject and citizen. Thomas Bernhard put it in a phrase that Pierre Bourdieu liked to quote: "The state forced me to enter it." All the rationality, or positivity, of the law can never erase the original violence of this compelled inclusion. The state's violence is rooted in the fact that it is obligatory to enter and impossible to get out. The state never gives one a choice. We are born in the state, seized by the state, and defined by the state. We are the objects of the state, subjugated to it. It imprisons us.

From the perspective of political theory, isn't the real question why there aren't more Snowdens or Assanges? These figures have made a break. Their actions are not typical: rejecting nationality and setting out for somewhere else represent uncommon attitudes. What does the rarity of such a bearing show, if not just how intensely we tend to stick to a sense of belonging that has occurred by force and to view it as our own—and to such an extent that we no longer question it and cannot even imagining doing without it?

The critique of the subject should start with the ontological condition of dispossession that all political facticity implies. Saying that we are born as legal subjects means saying we are constituted by the

foundational violence of forced inclusion, which can never be challenged: one can never contest one's nationality—not even Snowden
has managed to do so. He is still American, even though he resides in
Russia. As radical as his course of action is, he has no choice but to
struggle with the system of states and sovereignties and to play one
system against the other.

What is more, one aspect of Snowden's flight proves particularly
interesting. On 23 June 2013, during a stopover in Russia on the way
from Hong Kong to South America, Snowden was blocked from taking a plane because the United States had revoked his passport. This
administrative action forced him to remain in the transit area of the
Moscow airport with Sarah Harrison until 1 August, when the Rus-
sian government granted him temporary asylum. Many discussions
and analyses of this chain of events have occurred—especially about
the legality of the American government's decision to withdraw a
citizen's passport in this manner.[13] But over and above juridical questions, the situation reminds us that we all travel *on the condition that
the state authorizes us to do so*, or, better: *because the state has authorized us to do so*. In other words, in the capacity of citizens, we have
been subjugated to a state that exercises the right it has arrogated to
itself to forbid us to leave its territory.

Departure

In essence, an analysis of the state that affirms democratic demands
should lead to radicalized contractualism, making the question of
the "social contract" a contractual matter, too. Snowden and Assange
might offer a starting point for founding a radical politics that would
subject as many realities as possible to deliberation. Belonging to a
state should be rethought—in terms of choice, not constraint.

To be sure, this theoretical demand should make us ask about the
meaning of migratory practices that occur every day, often in silence
and on an individual scale. Interpreting migratory movements often

serves to depoliticize them. For the most part, they receive attention as forced displacements arising from economic factors, wars, and so on. As a rule, the reason for emigration is sought in need, necessity, obligation, and so forth. But couldn't migration also, and in contrast, be seen as a political gesture—and even a form of political expression?[14] When a subject migrates, isn't she or he performing a kind of coup d'état? Such movement makes states and legislative systems compete with each other. In other words, the migrant formulates a demand or, better still, exercises a kind of right to choose his or her nationality, his or her state, and claim for him- or herself control over the form and nature of the system of laws to observe. In this sense—and whatever motivation or intention is at work—the practice involves a democratic concern inasmuch as it suspends sovereignty by subjecting the state to the choice of the citizen (instead of the other way around).[15]

In seeking a new way to analyze the state as a form and the relationship of citizens to the nation and to sedition, inspiration may be drawn from traditions that have focused on the problem of the borders of political communities, or belonging that is, efforts insisting on how the call for democracy requires us to undo the hold that state structures exercise in order to affirm individuals' right to take leave of them.

At the end of *Civil Disobedience*, for instance, Thoreau remarks a kind of failure of civil disobedience as a practice. Consequently, he proposes another way of expressing dissent. Instead of confronting the state, he invokes the right not to be considered a member of a community to which he no longer has any formal ties. For Thoreau, the problematic nature of the state is rooted in its enclosure and in the attendant obligation to belong to it. A state that respects individual rights should leave room for the possibility of making an exit. It cannot possess a democratic form unless it accepts that individuals have the capacity to withdraw and gives up on forcing them to participate in a community they do not recognize as legitimate: "I please myself with imagining a state at last which can afford to be just to all men, and to treat the individual with respect as a neighbor; which even would not think it inconsistent with its own repose if a few were to live aloof from it."[16]

This idea returns in libertarian theory, particularly the works of Robert Nozick. Making the notion of force the center of reflection on the state, Nozick redefines the question of politics. Because the state represents an instance of constraint, it cannot have legitimacy unless individuals have *chosen* to belong to it. A genuinely liberal society cannot view the question of belonging as a matter of fact. It must be a matter of choice: a question of politics, not birth. As such, libertarian critique should be based on a redefinition of the state's organization: to be legitimate, it must take the form of a chosen association, that is, be "a world which all rational inhabitants may leave for any other world they can imagine."[17]

In libertarian society, belonging necessarily admits transformation. Ultimately, it must harbor a plurality of societies: "Each community must win and hold the voluntary adherence of its members. No pattern is *imposed* on everyone, and the result will be one pattern if and only if everyone voluntarily chooses to live in accordance with that pattern of community."[18] Nozick describes the society that the implementation of his principles would entail:

Imagine a possible world in which to live; this world need not contain everyone else now alive, and it may contain beings who have never actually lived. Every rational creature in this world you have imagined will have the same rights of imagining a possible world for himself to live in (in which all other rational inhabitants have the same imagining rights, and so on) as you have. The other inhabitants of the world you have imagined may choose to stay in the world which has been created for them (they have been created for) or they may choose to leave your world and inhabit a world of their own imagining. If they choose to leave your world and live in another, your world is without them. You may choose to abandon your imagined world, now without its emigrants. This process goes on; worlds are created, people leave them, create new worlds, and so on.[19]

Analyses like those of Thoreau and, in turn, Nozick, as well as the practices pursued by Snowden and Assange, entail the redefinition of political theory. They lead us to critique notions that often remain unquestioned and accepted as simple facts: cohabitation, community, and society. Cohabitation is not an ontological given. Nor are the communities we form with others just a given. They represent operations of power: forces of inclusion and exclusion bring them into existence and define their contours. The question of politics cannot be limited to analyzing the modes in which the polis is organized. It should bear on the polis itself, modes of collective "belonging," and therefore the right to enter—or refuse—such or such a group. To what extent would it be possible no longer to belong? What would this look like? With whom have I consented to enter an alliance? What would it mean to move beyond citizenship ? What would it mean to belong to democracy rather than to a state? Inasmuch as these questions remain unasked, no radical critique of state violence and the constitutional state in its current form can be carried out.

CHAPTER 6

ESCAPING CITIZENSHIP

POLITICIZING THE QUESTION OF BELONGING, giving oneself the right to flee, and encouraging a form of anonymity that enables the subject to act without being identified: these modes of action do not represent partial innovations. They do not simply enhance the ready array of forms of resistance—the kinds of collective mobilization available to us, at everyone's disposal. Rather, these modalities of revolt break with the political configuration of our day. They promote the emergence of subjectivities emancipated from prescribed and established forms of politics.

Liberal democracy is tied to a certain profile of the subject, which regulates our way of viewing ourselves both under "normal" conditions of everyday life and in times of struggle. The fact of being included within a state, of having been produced by our inscription within it, entails a certain self-understanding. As James C. Scott remarks at the end of *The Art of Not Being Governed*,[1] a book that examines conflicted relations between the nomad peoples of Southeast Asia and the state, the logic of the state and its order of law involve the logic of the proper name, signature, and identity. When an instance of political sovereignty is imposed on subjects, their constitution as legal subjects—that is, as subjects to a legal order—occurs by the imposition of stable, fixed, and recognizable identities. These same identities are imposed on the environment in which they live:

> Much early state-making seems to have been a process of naming units that were once fluid or unnamed: villages, districts, lineages, tribes, chiefs, families, and fields. The process of naming, when joined to the administrative power of the state, can create entities that did not previously exist. For Han Chinese officials, one distinguishing characteristic of "barbarians" was that they did not have patronyms. Such stable names were, among the Han themselves, the result of a much earlier exercise in state-making. In this sense, the very units of identity and place, which then acquire a distinctive genealogy and history, are, in their official, stable form, a state effect linked to writing.[2]

I am not sure that I completely subscribe to this analysis of politics and the state. It is based on a series of oppositions that are somewhat simplistic and involve picturing power as a unifying, ordering, and definitive instance; this, in turn, ties the analysis of power to an implicit narrative harboring something like a prepolitical condition characterized by fluidity, multiplicity, disorder, incoherence, and so on—which power then organizes, classifies, and fixes once and for all.

Scott is not alone in taking an approach shot through with spontaneity—far from it. Such a view is in evidence across the spectrum of modern thinking. For example, the works of the anthropologist Pierre Clastres, whom Scott enlists for his own project, present the state as a form that imposes unity, distinctions, and hierarchies on societies enjoying equality and transversality: "what the Savages exhibit is the continual effort to prevent chiefs from being chiefs, the refusal of unification, the endeavor to exorcise the One, the State."[3]

Strikingly, Foucault also uses this schema to understand not only the state but the operations of power in general. Indeed, *Discipline and Punish* portrays discipline as a technique of "ordering . . . a given multiplicity."[4] The contemporary management of illegalities and the workings of the penal system have the function of substituting, for the "vague, swarming mass of a population practising occasional illegality," a "relatively small and enclosed group of individuals on whom a constant surveillance may be kept"—"delinquents."[5]

Picturing the state—or power—as an instance that subdues an original plurality and introduces order where scattering once prevailed amounts, in my eyes, to disregarding the regimes of identification, stabilization, and arrangement that precede the state and legality. As we know, Gabriel Tarde, in a crucial polemic, faulted Émile Durkheim for opposing "homogeneous society" to "heterogeneous society" and observed that the societies one qualifies as homogeneous only look this way because one does not know or understand the principle of differentiation at work within them.[6] By the same token, describing power as an arrangement for ordering multiplicities means disregarding the principles of organization and unification that are already operative in what seems to be "multiple" and "swarming." Undoubtedly, then, it is necessary to avoid saying that power "unifies" or that it is what "introduces order." Still, this should not keep us from saying that legality means imposing certain, specific principles of unification.

Counter-Subjects

Being born in a constitutional state means being captured, from birth, within operations of power that are applied to us and define our existence: they constitute us as members of the political community, as beings protected by the law and the prohibitions it decrees. At the same time and in equal measure, however, we are established as responsible subjects and are supposed to answer for our actions—for which we risk punishment at the hands of judicial authority. Legal subjectivity arises from juridical techniques that enable an ensemble of behaviors to be linked to the same person, so that his or her duties toward others and sanctions applied to him or her have meaning. This is the sense of Hans Kelsen's celebrated formulation: "The so-called physical person . . . is not a human being, but the personified unity of the legal norms that obligate or authorize one and the same human being. It is not a natural reality but a legal construction, created by the science of law."[7] Thus, to be a legal subject—and, more still, to be a "citizen"—is to occupy the point where three constitutive forces intersect: nationality; incorporation into a certain juridico-political space and exercising the rights available there; and being susceptible to the logic of imputation and individual responsibility.

In this context, what strikes me as significant in the actions performed by Snowden, Assange, and Manning—in the struggles pursued by Anonymous and an organization such as WikiLeaks—is the aspiration to constitute subjectivity by escaping from the ways the state produces us and the framework that seizes us as soon as we enter the world. The point is not just to undo what, following Didier Eribon's notion of "social verdicts,"[8] one might call politico-juridical verdicts, but to try to live the experiences of which we are deprived by the fact of being fashioned as citizens. Snowden, Assange, and Manning incarnate counter-subjects with respect to the orders of citizenship and the law. They exhibit the will to reclaim a certain number of dimensions of existence. Constituting oneself as an anonymous subject means demanding the potential to act without being identified, without being held responsible for what one does. In other words, it means endeavoring to escape the way that power ties us to what we do. The practice of anonymity is inscribed within a movement that seeks to check—or even lift, however slightly—the mechanisms of subjugation. The goal is to free oneself from the order of the law, from attachment to it, from the weight of responsibility.

As such, the attitude of flight and sedition represents a spectacular, public act of refusing the operation of inclusion within a national community that the juridical order performs. Its objective is to call the notion of belonging into question—to attest to the will to make this matter one's own by interrogating the legitimacy of the forced inscriptions effected by legal authority.

In both cases, action bears on the same goal—or, more precisely, it is underpinned by the same intention: to regain a certain measure of control over oneself, to experience potentialities, modes of existence, and forms of action of which we were stripped when we acquired the status of legal subjects. The task is not just to question the framework within which the subject ordinarily develops but, more still, to invent a style of life outside this frame.

Life-or-Death

The state response to the actions of Snowden, Assange, and Manning has proven so violent because of the challenges they raise. The reaction has been brutal and unprecedented in proportion to the destabilization occasioned by these counter-subjects' emergence. To gauge the forces at work, one may seek an analogy in the aesthetic realm. I am thinking of Pierre Bourdieu's analysis of the Impressionist revolution and the relationship between Manet and the Academy of Fine Arts.

In this confrontation, Bourdieu observes, "Manet" and "academic art" stand for two different conceptions of the painter's function, two distinct kinds of artistic activity—in sum, two opposing ways that the field of art can function. Manet did not just introduce a new manner of painting. He also brought forth a new mode of subjectification: the life of the artist. As such, the Impressionist revolution was not merely an aesthetic revolution. It was also, at the same time, an ethical, symbolic, and political revolution—a matter of

entirely changing the vision of the world, the hierarchy of priorities, and the painter's function. The painter ceases to be a master and becomes an artist, the guarantor of himself. In this new system, one of the things to be invented is the new role of the painter as a figure with an extraordinary biography, who pours the whole of his being into his work and provides the object of celebration as a singular personality.[9]

Manet and the Academy were irreconcilable. The creator of *Déjeuner sur l'herbe* introduced a way of being that called into question the system of the fine arts as a whole:

The struggle Manet initiates is a battle for life or death. If the heresiarch wins, if he succeeds in imposing belief in what he does and what he is, the whole of the academic system will founder (and this is exactly what happened: within a few years, courses in *pompier* painting fell from the summits to less than nothing): no quarter is given. Manet mounted his attack on the very heart of academic art, such that—as the saying goes—it was "him or them."[10]

In the same fashion, the attack that Snowden, Assange, and Manning have mounted aims at the heart of the juridico-political system. They have brought forth a style of political life that calls into question the arrangements regulating the day-to-day operations of contemporary democracies. This is why there is every reason to believe that legal proceedings against them are less a matter of punishing the "crimes" that have supposedly been committed than of refashioning their authors as legal subjects who bear responsibility—reinscribing them in the legal order they have sought to take apart. "You're a traitor, you're a thief, you belong to the state. You should be loyal to your nation, you can't leave." In a word: "What you did didn't even happen. You're still what you pretend not to be: a citizen who must answer to the law."

The Future

Many works of history and critical theory have been devoted to traditions of defying the law, to figures of revolt against the state and its sovereign. Examples include Eric Hobsbawm's bandits, Christopher Hill's brigands, Daniel Heller-Roazen's pirates, and Jacques Derrida's rogues; one might also include the figure of Antigone, as analyzed by Hegel.[11] However, it does not strike me as exaggerated to declare that Snowden, Assange, and Manning represent something singular, a specific kind of combat. In this sense, we are witnessing the emergence of something new, not a reprise of long-standing tradition.

Indeed, it is worth noting that when rogues, bandits, pirates, and their like confront the state, they almost always do so in the name of the past: it is a matter of combating a legal order that is now asserting itself by appealing to a traditional and customary order that the new laws imperil. The task is to carve out space so that erstwhile ways of life will survive.

In contrast, the actions of Snowden, Assange, and Manning do not involve defying the law in the name of preexisting customs. They seek to play out new possibilities against the legal and political order as it now functions: to formulate new demands and bring to life new, unprecedented practices. Anonymous subjectification and the politicization of national belonging do not mean making all legal order impossible. Instead, they mean demanding the construction of a legal system that is more democratic and less violent, one that is anchored in the practical and theoretical deconstruction of the state, nation, and citizen as forms.

CHAPTER 7

DENATIONALIZING MINDS

IT MIGHT SEEM STRANGE that the topic of the Internet has hardly come up at all over the course of this book. Indeed, I have approached the stakes of the actions performed by Snowden, Manning, and Assange, the projects of Anonymous and WikiLeaks, struggles for protecting civil liberties against mass surveillance, and so on, without devoting detailed discussion to new technologies or the Web. It did not seem necessary for my argument.

And yet, we shouldn't avoid a concluding reflection on these subjects. More specifically, I would like to raise a problem that could be formulated in the following terms: is it an accident that the renewals I have analyzed here took place in the context of the Internet, within milieus invested in employing the technological tools that it offers? Is it possible to discern a connection between the Internet and the production of new social and political subjectivities?

To broach this field of problems, I would like to start with a relatively familiar observation but interpret it in a different way than usual: when reading about individuals caught up in the struggles of the Internet era, one often finds descriptions of solitary, bizarre, and

isolated beings. Typically, they are said not to have been fully integrated into groups of friends, to have lived in a kind of confinement.
Hackers, members of Anonymous, and geeks are portayed as "un-
sociable"; they do not interact with others, and they spend extended
periods in front of their computer screens.

Portraits of this type have been drawn of both Snowden and
Manning. Greenwald has described Snowden's psychic investment
in the Internet and underscored just how much Snowden's mental
universe developed within a virtual universe. The following passage
illustrates the kind of subjectivity associated with the Internet and
how it engenders specific modes of existence:

> Especially central to his worldview was the unprecedented value
> of the Internet. As for many of his generation, "the Internet" for
> him wasn't some isolated tool to use for discrete tasks. It was the
> place in which his *mind and personality* developed, a *place unto
> itself* that offered freedom, exploration, and the potential for in-
> tellectual growth and understanding.

Greenwald continues:

> To Snowden, the unique qualities of the Internet were incom-
> parably valuable, to be preserved at all costs. He had used the
> Internet as a teenager to *explore ideas and speak with people in
> faraway places and from radically different backgrounds* whom he'd
> never otherwise have encountered.

The author concludes by quoting Snowden himself: "Basically, the
Internet allowed me to experience freedom and explore my full capacity as a human being."[1]

We should, I believe, retain the emphasis that Greenwald and
Snowden place on the idea that the Internet is a "place unto itself,"

specifically one that offers individuals the possibility to "explore ideas" and "speak with people in faraway places and from radically different backgrounds." Even though there is always something a little naïve and utopian about that kind of thinking, it still points to extremely important stakes.

In fact, describing the Internet as a site of "exploration," "encounter," or "dialogue" means taking stock of one of the potentials this technology harbors: this virtual space can (I want to insist on the *potential*) provide a site of socialization that is an alternative to customary communities and, for this reason, help to redefine the relationship of individuals to "socialization" and "belonging."

Borders

In analyzing the genesis of the subject, the formation of subjectivity, one of the essential dimensions is the problem of borders, the psychic space in which one defines oneself. In effect, what sociologists call "socialization" unfolds in extremely codified circles that are imposed on the subject by virtue of where and when she or he happens to have been born. One's school, neighborhood, social class, family, and, to be sure, nation represent key elements of the framework of daily life. They constitute objective structures of experience that fashion one's mental space; they dictate what proves topical and vital— the subject's points of reference for self-definition. The process of socialization subjects me to the physical space in which I was born; through its mechanisms of incorporation, to employ Bourdieu's terminology, it transforms the objective structures in which I am held into subjective ones.

In this context, the question arises whether the Internet is capable of effecting a rupture with what these frameworks of socialization— which are both self-evident and a matter of imposition—force upon us. (I write *capable*, because, needless to say, this depends on how it is used, which varies by social class, age, gender, and so on.) In effect, spending extensive time on the Internet could provide the basis for learning to orient oneself differently in space, for understanding one's own position differently. In terms of the topography that is imposed on us, the Internet represents a counter-space for socialization—a space that escapes the a priori ties one is supposed to create and the milieus one is supposed to frequent. Political, musical, sexual, and playful interests (among other things) give rise to communities of discussion and exchange where individuals are able to feel closer and share more than in the physical or legal space they are *forced* to inhabit—with family, friends and acquaintances from their surroundings, colleagues, and so on.

As such, the Internet gives the subject the ability to practice what one might call a *chosen* socialization. Ultimately, the solitude or withdrawal that individuals who spend a great deal of time on the Internet display vis-à-vis family or school might just be a consequence of the fact that, after one has discovered a world of desired and chosen affinities, the confining nature of traditional cohabitation and socialization seems simply unbearable. This leads to a disinvestment from *that* world, *that* type of belonging, in order to join other circles.[2]

The Internet, then, contributes to a redefinition of the question of proximity and distance—the limits and borders placed on *who* it is one seeks to avoid or contact. It opens a path for taking distance from forced belonging—for freeing oneself and finding other groups. Belonging becomes a matter of choice, and one is less and less constrained by a sense of duty to associations that have been imposed—where, gradually, it is no longer possible to recognize oneself at all. The relationship between the Internet and the predisposition to flight, or "treason," may be explained by this process of dissolving traditional allegiances, which entails the right to choose the worlds one inhabits, or at least to leave them.

Imagination

In a classic historical study, Benedict Anderson insisted on the fact that "all communities larger than primordial villages of face-to-face contact (and perhaps even these) are imagined."[3] The borders of a group—ways of conceiving who it is with whom we form a community and who are those who are strangers to us—always arises from an imaginary or fantasmatic construction, the play of representations. Anderson links the origins of national consciousness—that is, both the birth of the idea of the nation and the symbolic construction of its limits—to the advent of a new technology: printing. By his account, printing enabled national languages to rise up against the domination of Latin, achieve codification, and, above all, to produce texts that then circulated in a fixed realm where something like a public sphere and a sense of shared reality emerged.[4] Hence the question: what if, in our own times, the Internet were contributing to the denationalization of minds and imaginaries? What if this technology enabled subjects to provide themselves a greater space of inscription and definition, come up with new ways of reinventing themselves, and (re)think the collectives of which they are a part? What would a politics look like that followed from these new modes of subjectification?

CONCLUSION

IN THE AMERICAN DEMOCRATIC TRADITION, the formula "We the people" symbolizes the classical conception of political activity. This proclamation, inscribed in the Constitution of the United States, is regularly and ritually taken up by protest movements—most recently, by Occupy.

"We the people," publicly invoked at an assembly, means asserting oneself as the people in possession of democratic legitimacy. It means putting popular sovereignty into play and laying claim to the right to speak and govern oneself in defiance of arbitrary institutions and negative powers—or even of the government itself, inasmuch as it takes measures that do not meet with the people's approval. As such, the formula ties political and democratic action to the performative construction of a community qua political community. Wholly in keeping with all theories of the social contract, it involves transforming a given group of individuals who are assembled—whether in a square or as a nation or state—into a *political* community that represents the site of democratic legitimacy and affirms the right to exercise it.

In this context, it seems to me that one may understand the political subjectivity that may be emerging through the Internet, as well as the technological potential it affords, by examining how a group like Anonymous conceives of the process of community formation to which it is contributing. Each one of the group's videos or interventions begins with a ritualized formula. Instead of "We the people," it declares, "Hello citizens of the world, we are Anonymous."

The interpellation "Hello citizens of the world, we are Anonymous" is intended for everyone. The group that is called on to come together is not fixed in advance by national borders. A priori, it is impossible to know who will take part or see him- or herself in this group. In consequence, politics no longer represents a gesture through which a given, predetermined collective takes form as a political community. This interpellation, of uncertain origin (no one knows who is saying "We the Anonymous") and uncertain address, aims to produce a new group—that is, to wrest individuals away from established modes of belonging and loyalty and have them join the "we" at hand, so that they will become part of a new kind of community engaging in struggle. In fact, the political entities that stand to be formed will never yield a "we." They will have no name. They will take the form of a provisional gathering of scattered and plural individuals who choose, at a certain moment in time and for their own reasons, to form an alliance. As such, the denationalization of minds does not culminate in anything like a worldwide commonality. Quite the opposite: it represents a single instance within a process of desubjugation from constrictive identifications, in order to liberate a capacity to imagine—and therefore establish—new communities that are plural, heterogeneous, and ephemeral.

Having the world as one's mental horizon; forging unprecedented, elective groups; and casting off all imposed belongings by means of politicizing how we stand inscribed in space and in relation to others: such, it may be, are the axes of the art of revolt that is emerging today—the achievement of men and women who define themselves as "citizens of the world."

NOTES

Introduction

1. Charles Tilly, *The Contentious French: Four Centuries of Popular Struggle* (Cambridge, MA: Belknap, 1986).

2. "He betrayed the United States and for that betrayal, he deserves to spend the majority of his remaining life in confinement," Army prosecutor Captain Joe Morrow said. *cbcnews* online (*The Associated Press*), 19 August 2013, http://www .cbc.ca/news/world/bradley-manning-s-prosecutors-seek -60-year-term-1.1378986.

3. "The Inhumane Conditions of Manning's Detention," a stupefying article by Glenn Greenwald, offers an account that almost beggars belief. *Salon*, 15 December 2010, http://www.salon.com/2010/12/15/manning_3/.

4. "US Calls Assange 'Enemy of State'" *The Sydney Morning Herald* online, 27 September 2012, http://www.smh.com.au/federal-politics/political-news/us -calls-assange-enemy-of-state-20120926-26m7s.

5. Wendy Brown, *Walled States, Waning Sovereignty* (New York: Zone, 2010).

6. Didier Eribon, *Michel Foucault*, trans. Betsy Wing (Cambridge, MA: Harvard University Press, 1992), 158–60.

Chapter 1

1. Quoted in Glenn Greenwald, *No Place to Hide: Edward Snowden, the NSA, and the U.S. Surveillance State* (New York: Picador, 2015), 23–24. Emphasis added.

2. The words are Snowden's own. Cf. Antoine Lefébure, *L'Affaire Snowden* (Paris: La Découverte, 2014), 30.

3. Julian Assange, "Internet est devenu le système nerveux de nos sociétés," *Philosophie Magazine*, June 2013. [Not available in English.] For a fuller view of Assange's thinking, see his eloquent exchange with Hans Ulrich Obrist, *e-flux* Journal #25 (May 2011): http://www.e-flux.com/journal/in-conversation-with-julian-assange-part-i/.

4. Julian Assange, with Jacob Appelbaum, Andy Müller-Maguhn, and Jérémie Zimmermann, *Cypherpunks: Freedom and the Future of the Internet* (New York: OR, 2012).

5. Julian Assange et al., *Cypherpunks,* 8–9.

6. "NSA Data Leaker Edward Snowden Says He Took No Secret Files to Russia," *UPI,* 18 October 2013, http://www.upi.com/Top_News/World-News/2013/10/18/NSA-data-leaker-Edward-Snowden-says-he-took-no-secret-files-to-Russia/99441382105192/

Chapter 2

1. Giorgio Agamben, *State of Exception,* trans. Kevin Attell (Chicago: University of Chicago Press, 2005), 3–4.

2. Judith Butler and Gayatri Chakravorty Spivak, *Who Sings the Nation-State? Language, Politics, Belonging* (New York: Seagull, 2007), 35.

3. Judith Butler, *Precarious Life: The Powers of Mourning and Violence* (New York: Verso, 2004).

4. Ibid., 66.

5. Noam Chomsky, "Edward Snowden, the World's 'Most Wanted Criminal,'" *Truthout,* 20 June 2014, http://www.truth-out.org/opinion/item/24071-noam-chomsky-edward-snowden-the-worlds-most-wanted-criminal.

Chapter 3

1. Giorgio Agamben, *Homo Sacer: Sovereign Power and Bare Life*, trans. Daniel Heller-Roazen (Stanford: Stanford University Press, 1998).

2. Jacques Derrida, *The Death Penalty*, trans. Peggy Kamuf (Chicago: University of Chicago Press, 2013).

3. Agamben, *Homo Sacer*, 174–75.

4. Agamben, *State of Exception*, 2–3.

5. Judith Butler, *Parting Ways: Jewishness and the Critique of Zionism* (New York: Columbia University Press, 2012), 21.

6. Ibid., 144–45.

Part 2

1. On the debates that critical theory brings to bear on the legal order and, more specifically, how the formal nature of liberal rights can be viewed as a source of

inspiration and invention for liberation movements, see Joan Wallach Scott, *Gender and the Politics of History* (New York: Columbia University Press, 1999), 199–222.

2. Thus, my approach stands in opposition to undertakings that pretend that all struggles derive from the same principle and can be approached by way of the same interplay of concepts (voice, disobedience, collectives, the common, people, and so on). Political thought requires starting with the specificity of struggles in order to call existing categories into question, not transforming every field of battle into a scene that is general and predetermined in terms of its form and stakes. See, for example, Sandra Laugier and Albert Ogien, *Le Principe démocratie* (Paris: La Découverte, 2014).

3. Michel Foucault and Noam Chomsky, *The Chomsky-Foucault Debate: On Human Nature* (New York: the New Press, 2006), 1–67.

4. Ibid., 48.

5. Ibid., 48–49.

6. Today, important efforts are being made to think about civil disobedience outside the framework of liberal democracy. See, in particular, Robin Celikates, "Democratizing Civil Disobedience," *Philosophy & Social Criticism* 42, no. 10 (March 2016).

7. Cf. Jacques Derrida, "The Laws of Reflection: Nelson Mandela, in Admiration," in *Psyche: Inventions of the Other, Volume II*, ed. Peggy Kamuf and Elizabeth Rottenberg (Stanford: Stanford University Press, 2008), 63–86.

8. John Rawls, *A Theory of Justice, Revised Edition* (Cambridge, MA: Harvard University Press, 1990), 320.

9. Ibid., 321.

10. Ibid.

11. Ibid.

12. Ibid., 322.

13. Henry David Thoreau, *The Portable Thoreau* (New York: Penguin, 2012), 86.

14. Balázs Bodó, "You Have No Sovereignty Where We Gather—WikiLeaks and Freedom, Autonomy and Sovereignty in the Cloud," *Social Science Research Network*, March 2011: 4–5, *http://www.a51.nl/*storage/pdf/SSRN_id17805191.pdf.

Chapter 4

1. Frédéric Bardeau and Nicolas Danet, *Anonymous* (Paris: FYP Éditions, 2014), 99.

2. Bardeau and Danet, *Anonymous*, 113. On the plurality of practices and identities grouped under this title, see the indispensable study by Gabriela Coleman, *Hacker, Hoaxer, Whistleblower, Spy: The Many Faces of Anonymous* (London: Verso Books, 2014).

3. Bardeau and Danet, *Anonymous*, 99.

4. Jürgen Habermas, *Between Facts and Norms: Contributions to a Discourse Theory of Law and Democracy*, trans. William Rehg (Cambridge, MA: MIT Press, 1998).

5. Eric Hobsbawm, *Bandits* (New York, Pantheon, 1981).

6. Hannah Arendt, *The Human Condition* (Chicago: University of Chicago Press, 1998), 63.

7. Ibid., 198–99.

8. Albert O. Hirschman, *Exit, Voice, and Loyalty: Responses to Decline in Firms, Organizations, and States* (Cambridge, MA: Harvard University Press, 1970).

9. Judith Butler, "So What Are the Demands? And Where Do They Go from Here?," *Tidal. Occupy Theory Occupy Strategy*, no. 2 (March 2012). See also Butler, "Bodies in Alliance and the Politics of the Street," a lecture delivered in Venice (2011): European Institute for Progressive Cultural Politics, *Transversal Texts* (September 2011), http://www.eipcp.net/transversal/1011/butler/en, as well as Butler, *Notes Toward a Performative Theory of Assembly* (Cambridge, MA: Harvard University Press, 2016).

10. Balázs Bodó, "You Have No Sovereignty Where We Gather—Wikileaks and Freedom, Autonomy and Sovereignty in the Cloud" (March 7, 2011). Available at SSRN: https://ssrn.com/abstract=1780519 or http://dx.doi.org/10.2139/ssrn.1780519

11. Joan W. Scott, "Fantasy Echo: History and the Constrution of Identity," *Critical Inquiry* 27.2 (2001): 284–304.

12. Didier Eribon, *Principes d'une pensée critique* (Paris, Fayard, 2016). See, especially, the essay "Vies hantées."

13. Bodó, "You Have No Sovereignty Where We Gather," 6.

14. Michel Foucault, *Wrong-Doing, Truth-Telling: The Function of Avowal in Justice*, trans. Stephen W. Sawyer (Chicago: University of Chicago Press, 2014).

15. Hannah Arendt, *The Human Condition*, 63–67.

16. Georg Simmel, *Conflict and the Web of Group-Affiliations*, trans. Kurt H. Wolff (New York: The Free Press, 1964).

17. Cf., especially, Axel Honneth, *The Pathologies of Individual Freedom*, trans. Ladislaus Löb (Princeton: Princeton University Press, 2010).

Chapter 5

1. Greenwald, *No Place to Hide*, 113–14.

2. Cf. Charles Beitz, *Political Theory and International Relations* (Princeton: Princeton University Press, 1979).

3. John Rawls, *The Laws of Peoples: With "The Idea of Public Reason Revis-*

ited" (Cambridge, MA: Harvard University Press, 2001), 86. See also Rawls, *A Theory of Justice*, 7.

4. Butler, *Parting Ways,* 23.

5. Ibid., 24.

6. Ibid., 129–30.

7. Max Weber, *Economy and Society: An Outline of Interpretive Sociology,* ed. Guenther Roth and Claus Wittich (Berkeley: University of California Press, 1978), 32.

8. Jacques Derrida, *Rogues: Two Essays on Reason,* trans. Pascale-Anne Brault and Michael Naas (Stanford: Stanford University Press, 2005), esp. 64–65.

9. Cf. Carrie Dann, "Kerry: Snowden a 'Coward' and 'Traitor,'" *NBC News* online, 28 May 2014, http://www.nbcnews.com/politics/first-read/kerry-snowden -coward-traitor-n116366.

10. Jean-Paul Sartre, "Materialism and Revolution," in *Literary and Philosophical Essays,* trans. Annette Michelson (New York: Collier Books, 1962).

11. Hirschman, *Exit,* 109.

12. Édouard Louis, *The End of Eddy* (New York: Farrar, Straus and Giroux, 2017).

13. Cf. Patrick Weil, "Citizenship, Passports, and the Legal Identity of Americans: Edward Snowden and Others Have a Case in the Courts," *The Yale Law Journal* 123 (23 April 2014).

14. For another way of thinking about escaping as a right, linked to an economic logic more than a democratic claim, cf. Sandro Mezzadra, "The Right to Escape," *Ephemera*, vol. 4/3: 267–75, http://www.ephemerajournal.org/sites/default /files/4-3mezzadra.pdf.

15. On the political force of taking flight and migration, viewed from a somewhat different perspective, see Édouard Louis, "Savoir-souffrir," *NRF* 609 (September 2014): 132–33.

16. Thoreau, *The Portable Thoreau*, 97.

17. Robert Nozick, *Anarchy, State, and Utopia* (Oxford: Blackwell, 1999), 299.

18. Ibid., 316.

19. Ibid., 299.

Chapter 6

1. James C. Scott, *The Art of Not Being Governed: An Anarchist History of Upland Southeast Asia* (New Haven: Yale University Press, 2009).

2. Ibid., 229.

3. Pierre Clastres, *Society Against the State: Essays in Political Anthropology*, trans. Robert Hurley (New York: Zone, 2007), 218.

4. Michel Foucault, *Discipline and Punish: The Birth of the Prison*, trans. Alan Sheridan (New York: Vintage, 1995), 149.

5. Ibid., 278.

6. Gabriel Tarde, *Monadology and Sociology*, trans. Theo Lorenc (Melbourne: re.press, 2012).

7. Hans Kelsen, *Pure Theory of Law* (Berkeley: University of California Press, 1978), 174. See also Marcela Iacub, *Penser les droits de la naissance* (Paris: PUF, 2002), 94–97.

8. Didier Eribon, *La Société comme verdict* (Paris, Fayard, 2013).

9. Pierre Bourdieu, "La révolution impressionniste," *Noroit* 303 (September–October 1987): 3–18.

10. Ibid.

11. Christopher Hill, *Liberty Against the Law* (London: Penguin, 1998); Daniel Heller-Roazen, *The Enemy of All: Piracy and the Law of Nations* (New York: Zone, 2009).

Chapter 7

1. Glenn Greenwald, *No Place to Hide*, 103; emphasis added.

2. Recently, Leo Bersani has dedicated a considerable amount of reflection to the practices of hiding and disappearance as ways to place systems of power and naming in crisis. See his *"Illegitimacy" in Thoughts and Things* (Chicago: University of Chicago Press, 2015).

3. Benedict Anderson, *Imagined Communities: Reflections on the Origin and Spread of Nationalism* (London: Verso, 2006), 6.

4. Ibid., 34–35.

104149

Lightning Source UK Ltd.
Milton Keynes UK
UKOW04f0336030817
306590UK00001B/128/P